This Beats Working For a Living

THIS

BEATS WORKING FOR

A LIVING

The Dark Secrets of a College Professor

by

Professor X

ARLINGTON HOUSE · · · · · · · · *New Rochelle, N.Y.*

Library of Congress Catalog Card Number 72–91218

ISBN 0–87000–189–2

MANUFACTURED IN THE UNITED STATES OF AMERICA

DEDICATED TO

Hubert H. Humphrey

WHO, AFTER LOSING IN 1968, BECAME A PROFESSOR—AND
THEREBY PROVED THE CORRECTNESS OF MY VOTE FOR

RICHARD NIXON,

AND TO

L. R. N.

FOR MAKING IT FUN.

Table of Contents

7

8

FOREWORD, PREFACE, AND INTRODUCTION

In years past the professor held a place of high esteem in America. True, there always was an undercurrent of ridicule associated with the breed; the "absent-minded professor" was the butt of many a joke, a fit topic for ridicule, the subject of immediate laughter in movies, books, and stage presentations. Politicians generally could pick up a few votes among less-educated audiences by making fun of academicians. For example, James E. "Pa" Ferguson in running for governor of Texas in 1918 centered his whole campaign on a fight with the University of Texas. He derisively told of one University professor who had spent two years in an attempt to grow wool on an armadillo's back. He called the faculty "butterfly chasers," "day dreamers," "educated fools," "liars," and "two-bit thieves," and he predicted that someday other nations would be raising armies to put down the University "autocracy"—unless, of course, he was elected and crushed the power of the professors quickly. Yet underneath the public ridicule the American people gener-

9

ally believed that professors really were kindly and lovable, that they had wisdom and could impart it to youth who in turn would use it to get jobs. The professor, like the preacher and the public school teacher, was supposed to have little thought of worldly possessions and thus was poorly paid, but he was a good man! Underneath that crusty, distracted, lost-in-thought exterior was a soft-hearted individual.

Then suddenly came the mid-1960s, and the public became more and more aware that taxes for higher education had become astronomical. That state budgets were strained to the limit supporting higher and yet higher salaries for college professors and for their nonsensical research. In fact, the public learned that colleges and universities were demanding—and getting—billions of dollars from the federal government in addition to what they were receiving from the states, and this while tuition was skyrocketing until few poor boys could afford to go to college. This awareness dawned just at a time when students were burning, bombing, and rioting—and some professors were visibly exhorting and even leading them on. Suddenly public opinion turned against college and university instructors, labeling the entire breed as fuzzy-headed liberals. One well-known Dixie third-party candidate for the presidency in 1968 caught this mood and drew wild cheers when he threatened to throw all pointy-headed professors' briefcases in the Potomac River.

Unfortunately for the state of higher education, the public has had good reason to believe the worst about professors, not because most of them are wild-eyed radicals bent on overthrowing the system but rather because too few of them have anything to profess. The Ph.D. has become a license to steal, inasmuch as the position of college instructor demands little

10

work, less intelligence, and no courage. In the words of some of my old Marine Corps friends, "They ought to be so ashamed that they should back up in the pay line." They certainly are not earning those high salaries.

Most professors would flunk the Chamber of Commerce test: they have "never met a payroll." What really is sad, however, is that so few of us ever have been on any payroll other than one at a college or university; that is, most of us have never held a job outside the academic community. Thus too many of us have an adolescent attitude toward the world, knowing almost nothing about the real world of business, government, and the arts. I have met few professors whom I would hire to run a peanut stand, let alone be the guardian of wisdom and Western civilization. The best cure for this dreadful situation would be to require college professors to earn their living at least one year out of every five by some means other than through teaching at an institution of higher learning. But if such a proposition ever became law, most of them would starve.

I set out here to write a sort of "Everything You Always Suspected About Professors, But Were Afraid To Ask For Fear It Would Be True." I hoped to write satire *but with the bite of truth*. I did this from my dozen and a half years as spectator and participant in the great swindle we call college teaching. Thus I have made up none of the anecdotes that follow; everything contained herein I have seen or heard—or at least have from good secondary sources.

And it is eminently fitting that this book should be published behind a mask of anonymity, for it dwells in several places on the cowardliness of professors and professing. In a community as close-knit as that of so-called scholars today, anonymity is necessary for me because I want to keep my job—and I might

11

just starve to death if I had to earn my living some other way. I repeat, courage is neither a virtue among academicians nor is it a way to continue at what certainly beats working for a living.

PROFESSOR X
September 1, 1972

This Beats Working For a Living

I

ACADEMIC DUTIES

WORK LOAD

I heard recently of a meeting of a legislative committee concerned with setting a budget for the coming year for the colleges and universities in that state. During the course of the hearings, the chairman of the committee questioned the president of one school about the work load of the professors at that institution, for, as everywhere, the impression he had was that the professors worked very little. "And how many hours do your professors teach?" the chairman asked. "Twelve," replied the president. "Well," responded the legislator, his voice filled with relief, "that's good. I think twelve hours a day is enough for anyone to work."

The college president wisely said nothing to correct the legislator's misconception. Actually what the president was saying was that his instructors taught *twelve hours a week*. This is probably a good national average for the amount of time a professor spends in the classroom—remembering that the college hour is only fifty minutes long. Thus, technically speaking, a college instructor with a twelve-hour load is in the classroom just ten sixty-minute hours each week. The fifty-minute hour originated in order to give the students ten minutes to get between classes.

At junior colleges, small state institutions, and most small private schools, the normal teaching load is fifteen hours per week. College professors still speak in horrified tones of the bad old days when eighteen and even twenty-one hours were required at some institutions. The larger state and private universities have the twelve-hour load, while a very few of the most prestigious institutions have only a nine-hour load, with a few of the most senior professors teaching only six (or even in rare instances) three hours per week. Thus a handy way to determine the prestige-level to be accorded a professor is to ask (as frequently is done at conventions), "What's a normal load at your school?"

Obviously professors have other duties that keep them busy during the rest of the hours they are on campus. When asked to explain how they fill their time, they note such things as preparing lectures, grading, reading, researching, and even writing. In some of these areas there are directives from the college administration; for example, professors are told to keep office hours, generally three to five hours a week, when they are available for student conferences. Too often, however, the professor is not in his office during these posted hours; he is visiting friends in other offices, having coffee in the student union, or simply not on campus.

In the other areas that are supposed to fill his time, the professor (as noted in the sections describing these activities) spends very little energy revising his lectures or grading or researching

16

or writing—or even reading. Especially not reading in his own field of specialty. He may have a book handy, but it probably is a murder mystery or science fiction or, if he has pretensions of culture, the latest novel recommended by *Saturday Review*. The books and articles in his own field are generally dull—and to read them both puts him to sleep and reminds him that he should be doing something. And finally there is committee work, which is endless in the college world. The professor complains endlessly about the committees on which he is forced to serve, but he brings this on himself; by demanding democratic government of the university, he forces the administration to create ever more committees (see the section about committees).

The professor, in truth, finds only some fifteen to twenty hours of his week filled with actual work related to his duties. Some of them, especially if they live in a city large enough to grant them some anonymity, take a part- or even full-time job off campus; and this is not moonlighting—it is daylighting. At one large Southwestern university at which I was teaching, a new Dean of the School of Business and Public Affairs almost had a mutiny on his hands when he decreed that no professor could hold a full- or even part-time job off campus without written permission from his office. He issued this decree when he learned that more than half his faculty was working downtown, not at night to earn a little extra pay, but during regular business hours. A few of his really good faculty members who had been doing this and who had learned that they could succeed in the real world promptly quit, while the poor ones slunk back to school and gave up all touch with what was happening outside those portals.

Other professors, those not so ambitious, do not try to moonlight or daylight. They become proficient at golf or bridge, or just go home and pet their dogs. A member of my department at that same Southwestern university, a bachelor, probably spent more time with his five dogs than he did at his duties at school; in fact, most of his time at the office was spent complaining about how overworked he was.

There are a few professors—human nature being what it is, probably about fifteen to twenty percent—who try to research and write, who really try to work with their students and to keep abreast of their fields, and thus who work forty, fifty, and even sixty hours a week. I have observed that the man truly successful in his field, who gains a reputation for excellent teaching and for wide publication, generally works twelve to fifteen hours a day and much of his weekends. Perhaps this explains the high divorce rate among the really successful academicians.

The college teacher thus can be among the world's laziest people, drawing his salary under false pretenses while complaining about being overworked and underpaid, or he can be among the world's hardest working individuals. Efficiency experts would not be welcomed on most campuses, however, for the majority of professors would be too embarrassed at their findings.

As to salaries for this work load, professors are amazingly well paid. I should preface my remarks about salary by noting that the good professor is underpaid at any salary, while the poor one is overpaid no matter what he receives. The problem is that they both—good and bad—are paid about the same. Today an average starting salary for someone with a master's degree and no experience is about $8,500. The beginning Ph.D. now can expect and usually receive about $11,000 as a starting salary. Of course, the rate of pay will vary from region to region in this country, but these are pretty good averages. Yet it should be noted that the figures quoted above are not for twelve months, but only for the school year of nine months. For teaching in the summer the professor generally can earn the other three months' salary.

At the upper end of the salary scale, junior colleges generally pay less. Their highest salaries will be somewhere in the vicinity of $15,000, while colleges and universities will average about $18,000 at this time. Again there are regional variations, just as there are certain prestigious institutions where maximum salaries run as high as $40,000 to $50,000 for top-name professors with no administrative duties, and who, naturally, teach only three or six hours.

Yet in talking about academic salaries, the sad part is that there often is no visible connection between pay and merit. Everyone marches together in virtual lockstep, the lazy getting raises of about the same size as the hard-working. Merit too often is not rewarded, nor is demerit penalized. All are supposed to get something each year simply because September 1st is the anniversary of the last pay raise. I look around here at this university and see, as at every other institution where I have worked, little visible difference between the salaries of twenty-five-year veterans who are unproductive and twenty-five-year veterans who have worked.

When a legislature in some particular state begins to talk about holding professors accountable for the money they receive—that is, to demand merit in return for annual pay raises —professors speak of them in tones once reserved to describe Hitler's storm troopers.

I suppose what I am saying in all this is that professors really are like too many other Americans. They want more and more pay for less and less work. The amount of work professors do—or should I say the amount of nonwork they do—was summarized recently by a vice president of a large Midwestern university. He was talking with his director of educational television, who was producing a magazine-style series for airing over the state educational television network. The vice president for academic affairs suggested that the director should do a program entitled "A Day in the Life of a University Professor," for, said the vice president, too few legislators or the public understood exactly what a professor did. "Take a camera and follow some professor around for a day shooting film, and you should be able to come up with a pretty good program," he advised. Then he paused for a moment, thought seriously, and concluded, "No, follow one around for a week, and you might be able to get enough film to make it look like one of them works hard for one day."

SELECTION OF TEXTBOOKS

A cliche, often repeated by old hands to young instructors, is that the way to teach any course is to select three textbooks: one for the students, one to take lectures from, and the third to take tests from. And as with all cliches, there is an element of truth in this statement. In any course there usually is no shortage of textbooks from which to choose, especially in those courses with large enrollments. Thus the task of selecting a textbook is far more difficult in those courses the young instructor is likely to teach—the basic introductory survey courses. In my field of history, for example, there must be at least thirty different textbooks for the American history survey courses that freshmen in many states are required to take. Few of these contain significant variations; as a politician said in 1968 of the two major political parties, "There's not a dime's worth of difference."

The professor has no difficulty in seeing the many specimens of textbooks. In the larger universities, college travelers (salesmen) for the textbook companies visit him at least once a semester, at which time they hawk their wares by offering to send examination copies. At the smaller schools, which the travelers rarely reach, the copies simply arrive through the mail. Not only the basic textbooks but also related monographs are sent to the professors in the hope that these also will be adopted. Thus every professor is able to build a reputable library at little or no expense. Those textbooks just keep coming.

And they provide a small source of income for some professors inasmuch as used-textbook companies purchase copies. Many a professor I know once or twice a year gathers all the free textbooks he has received and sells them, pocketing some fifty to one hundred dollars. The major publishers are becoming more and more aware of this practice, which basically is dishonest; they are aware that some professors ask for sample copies of everything, pretending they want the books to examine for possible adoption, in order to sell them. Thus more and more of the publishers are stamping "Not for Resale" in bold red ink across the top and bottom of complimentary copies of their books.

Once the professor has gathered sample copies of possible textbooks for his course, he has the choice of selection. Rarely is this done on the basis of the salesmanship of the college traveler employed by the publisher. The traveler cannot make a hard sell; his is the softest sell in salesmanship. He can buy a lunch or two, he can try to win friends, and he can try very slyly

21

to build a psychological obligation. But he cannot know what will result in a sale—for often the professor himself does not know why he selects one textbook over another. Obviously if one of the instructor's major professors (from his graduate school) has written the book, he will adopt it in order to be able to drop the author's name. Perhaps he has only met the author once at a convention and can do the same. But no one knows what makes professors adopt textbooks.

Certainly it is not the readability of the book that counts. In fact, I have observed that the more literary (readable) a book is, the less likely it is to be adopted. I think that intuitively professors shy away from well-written books because they realize that their lectures suffer by comparison. Or else they have taken their lectures from the well-written textbook and thus do not want the students ever to see it. Cribbing lectures from textbooks is more widespread than many people would suspect, although obviously it is intellectually dishonest.

Generally the textbook finally selected has not been read completely by the professor—nor will it be by the students. More than anything else it will be selected on the basis of the image of the author. You see, the big names in any discipline get an image, and here I mean politically and socially. Inasmuch as most professors are liberal, they select textbooks written by men with a liberal image. Therefore textbooks are selected more for the man writing them than for what he has written. The result is that most of them are wretchedly written, dull, ponderous—and liberal. The students' salvation resides in the fact that most do not read the things, and few of the remainder understand what they have read.

22

THE LECTURE

Traditionally, all a college professor needed in order to do his job in the classroom was a blackboard, some chalk, perhaps a map or two, and the ability to talk. Or, in many instances, simply to read what he had written out in his lecture notes. Professorial long-windedness has become legendary; in fact, doctors refer to cancerous growths on the vocal cords as "Professor's Nodes." Jestingly I have heard it said that if you ask a professor the time of day it takes him fifty minutes (the length of the average college class) to tell you.

The lecture is supposed to be a distillation of all that is pertinent on some particular aspect of the professor's specialty. He breaks down his course, be it ancient history or applied physics, into topics or units and lectures on each until the student understands it. Then he moves on to the next. The lecture is composed out of the professor's own training, his reading, his research, and his conclusions. At least, such is the theory. In truth, the professor most often makes up his lectures by assembling several textbooks for that particular subject and cribbing a little here and a little there. He does this if he is conscientious; the lazy simply do it from one textbook—even to the extent of simply xeroxing the text page for page. This type of professor considers himself hard-working if he types the material verbatim from the text rather than xeroxing it. I even have known a few too lazy to type the material and too cheap to pay for copying it and who, as a result, simply cut the pages out of the textbook, punched holes in the pages, and inserted them in a notebook. Professors sometimes joke that "Research is copying from several sources; plagiarism is copying from just one source." And many a professor who screams at his students for being guilty of plagiarism has secured his entire lecture notes just that way.

In fact, there probably is no area of more abysmal ignorance among college professors—and that is a mouthful of a statement —than the laws against plagiarism. Within the past year I was serving on a committee dealing with the problem of giving courses by closed-circuit television on campus when the question of copyright came up. The university's legal counsel said the issue was simple; everything would be copyrighted in the university's name. I responded that such a step would mean that the instructor who agreed to do television thereby could not use those same lectures off-campus even for an extension course without getting the university's permission, else he would be violating the copyright laws. Eventually the committee voted that the material would be copyrighted in the university's name but that the instructor would retain the right to use the material in his lectures and for purposes of publication in any noncompeting way.

During the course of this discussion, one lady professor of home economics exclaimed that she did not realize the extent of protection afforded by the copyright laws. "But I simply take all my lectures from other textbooks. Do you mean to tell me that I am violating the copyright laws?"

There in a nutshell simultaneously was demonstrated professorial laziness and ignorance. Nor was this home economics professor alone in the practice of cribbing her lectures from some textbook not assigned to the students; she was just the one naive enough to admit the practice openly. If the truth was known, several others in that same room were guilty of the practice—no doubt equally ignorant of their violation of the copyright laws.

But all of them were aware of the intellectual dishonesty of the practice. Every professor who cribs his lectures from a textbook or directly from other printed books does this with full awareness that he should be writing the lectures himself. He steals knowingly—yet will scream in indignation at a student who does the same thing for a term paper.

His lecture notes written (or copied), the professor then goes into the classroom to deliver them—all too often in a dull, dry monotone. Today, however, he finds the students restive with this approach. Television and movies have accustomed them to a more dynamic presentation; they find even the professor's most sparkling ideas of little interest, while his normal lectures are of value only to an insomniac. Fifty years ago the college instructor could be far from dynamic and yet be liked and respected by his students because he was opening new horizons for them. The professor who today would be great is one who combines wisdom with good stage presence. In short, he has to be half ham.

This point was driven home to me early in my career when a professor noted for his excellent lectures gave me his secret. "I tell them a joke," he said, "and then they tune in to listen. Then quickly, before they tune me out, I teach them something. When they start to tune out again, I tell another joke and pull their attention back. And so on." Unfortunately I do not know sufficient jokes suitable for the classroom to be that kind of lecturer; nor do most other professors have such a store of wit at their mental fingertips, and thus we continue to be deadly dull.

Because most professors do suffer by comparison with television and the movies, and because most of them know intuitively that their lectures are bad, they respond by blindly denouncing the caliber of their students. Thus faculties of bad teachers pass rules that are, in effect, handy clubs with which to beat students into attending their classes. For example, at most universities three unexcused absences from class result in the lowering of the student's final grade by one letter, six in lowering the grade two letters, and so on. The student with more than twelve unexcused absences cannot get any grade other than an F. Actually any student who can pass a course without attending class should be allowed to do so—and even be congratulated for his ability. In facing classes, I have found that students easily divide into three categories: those who will pass in spite of me (that is, can pass without attending class); those who sit there with the attitude, "I'm here, but I dare you to teach me anything"; and those whom I can help. I thank God for the latter and forget the other two categories—and sleep pretty well at night and have no ulcers.

The other escape for poor lecturers is to search desperately for new teaching methods to replace their dull lectures. Catchwords about lectures come frequently, have a brief vogue in the academic community, and then fade quickly—to be replaced by some new slogan-word. For example, a few years ago everyone was talking about "Excellence" as if it was a mythological beast that could be trapped and placed on display at the front gate of the college. Then came "Relevance," also to be trapped and put on display. In just a few short years we will have an entire zoo of such beasts—and the students still will be sleeping through our lectures. "We must have excellence!" thunder the sloganeers, and "We must be relevant!" There is no definition of just what relevance and excellence are. It is as if these were some new deity to be accepted on faith and to which we must build a shrine and worship.

A favorite way for the bad lecturer to abdicate his responsibility, especially if he is lazy, is to assign lectures to the students. In a class of twenty students, he tells them each will be required to give a twenty-five-minute presentation on some topic—and that fills ten lectures. In fact, if he gets a sufficiently large enrollment and assigns long lectures to the students, they will teach the whole class.

Another form of avoiding giving lectures is for the professor simply to abdicate. Those using this approach let the students decide what they want to study or discuss no matter what the formal title of the course is. An instructor in philosophy at my present university recently told a class, "I don't know what this course is supposed to be about. Therefore this semester we will talk about what you (the students) wish to discuss." The result, when professors fail to profess, is that students simply pool their ignorance.

A new innovation for those who do not have the ability to lecture their subject in an interesting way is a thing called "Individualized Programmed Instruction," obviously known as I.P.I. The instructor using this approach is supposed to break down his course into levels of goals, each to be achieved successively. If he has, for example, some thirty steps through which he hopes to lead the student, then he individualizes them and enumerates under each how the student is to show progress through that step to the next. The end result of using I.P.I. is that the students teach themselves the course, and thus the professor does not have to teach at all. We had a recent dose of this at my present institution—and I must say it achieved for its chief proponent what he wanted; the leader in the I.P.I. movement here got a deanship, and thus no longer has to teach. Perhaps I.P.I. can be used to advantage in some of the sciences and engineering courses, but in the Liberal Arts (the so-called Mystery Disciplines) it is difficult, if not impossible, to conceptualize where we intend to lead the students, or even what concepts we hope they will understand. Thus I.P.I. will never be a substitute for a good lecture.

And for those who do not wish to teach but who want to find a way, there always is the audio-visual approach. Get a film! Use a tape! Show some slides! In fact, pushing upward from the public schools is the hardware approach to teaching. Anytime the teacher wishes to show he is striving to be a better instructor, he submits a requisition for some piece of machinery: slide projector, tape recorder, closed-circuit television, movie projector. One of the major causes for the increasing cost of education in the United States is the delusion—foisted by poor teachers and salesmen of electronic hardware—that machines can produce better education. I say again, there is no substitute for a good lecture. All the machinery in the world will not make a dull lecture more sparkling, and all the machinery in the world is superfluous in a good lecture.

The principal reason for poor lectures is sheer laziness on the part of the professor. Anyone who has been through graduate school is competent to compile decent, passable lectures; every graduate student suffers through a sufficient number of poor lectures to be aware of what a good one is. Another and more common form of laziness is the professor who, when young, organized lectures—and then never changed them again. In 1959, when I was yet in graduate school, the instructor in a course in diplomatic history was reading along in his notes to the class and informed us: "And in San Francisco they now are working to form a United Nations." Looking up into our startled faces, he blandly commented, "These notes were written in

28

1944." And he went right on reading! On another occasion this same professor, a graybeard full of honors, was droning on when he came to the bottom of the page of one of his lectures; turning the page, he was reading on an entirely different subject. Again without the least embarrassment or hesitation, he informed us, "Here seven pages of my lecture notes are missing." And again he went right on reading as if nothing was amiss!

This same instructor once loaned his lecture notes to one of my fellow graduate students, who informed me that the professor had typed his jokes into his lectures (they were poor jokes at best)—and also underneath each jest had typed, "Ha Ha Ha Ha" all across the page. The old man not only had written in his jokes; he also had written in the laughter.

The failure to update lectures owing to laziness is rarely this flagrant, but the practice is widespread. I sometimes believe that the reason employers have lined up to hire college graduates in the spring (at least they have in the past) is not for anything the students might know—they do have little enough knowledge, and often it takes an employer six months to a year to train the new employee to the point where he is profitable to the company. The reason they hire college graduates is because the student, by staying in college for four years, has demonstrated an ability to survive while gutting out a bad situation. Not only does the student who graduates have to sit in a diversity of classes under a diversity of professors, but also he has to do a certain amount of work for each. The graduates of such a system probably will do all right in the business world, for there also they will have a diversity of bosses where they will have to gut out the situation and do a certain amount of work. In this sense, college is excellent training for life under our system of business and government. And, of course, those who fail to perform too well in college—and thus are really not suited to work in the business community—can always become teachers or government employees. So everyone gets a job.

Finally, in discussing the lecture, I would make one last point. When students fail, the tendency is for them to blame the professor. Deans and other administrators likewise tend to blame instructors for all student failures. However, the teaching-learning situation is a two-way street. Both professor and student have obligations: the professor to master his subject and to present it in the most interesting and learnable form; the student to read, study, question, and think. When both work, learning results. And learning is work! No learning takes place —just as no ditch gets dug—without work. Mental sweat is required of the student who would master some discipline. There are some student failures that can be attributed directly to professorial failure, but just as often they are from student failure. Perhaps in summation I might observe that both professor and student are human—and therefore tend to be lazy.

Nor does the professor really need to know anything about a specific subject to teach it. Several times I have had to teach a course involving some specialty about which I knew nothing. At the university level, teaching a course is slightly more difficult than it is in the public schools, where the educationist's slogan is "Give me the textbook and let me stay one chapter ahead and I can teach anything." In college, when a professor has to teach such a course, he finds the xerox machine his salvation—let him copy one chapter ahead and he can lecture anything. I once was approached by a department head from a well-known Western university about teaching economic history at his institution. "But my field is Western American history," I protested. "That's all right," he informed me with the wisdom of his experience.

"You can fake it until you learn it." Too many professors "fake it" for years—and never learn it either.

There is one salvation for the lecturer, which I learned the hard way. When I first was hired as a graduate student to lecture two sections of American history, I was petrified with fear as I approached my first lecture. The department head stopped me just as I was going to that first class. "Scared?" he asked. I replied that I was, whereupon he comforted me with this thought: "Don't be scared. They're just freshmen." I was relieved, for I read in this statement the thought that freshmen were callow and ill-informed and that I would know more than they did. Weeks later I told the department head how he had helped me. "But I didn't mean that at all," he said. "I meant that freshmen tend to be very forgiving." So are all college students, else most professors would be dismal failures.

EDUCATIONAL TELEVISION

When a professor walks into his classroom, closes the door, and begins to lecture, only he and his students know what kind of job he is doing. Most professors are wrong in thinking the students are really too ignorant or inexperienced to be able to judge their competence. The students do know, but inasmuch as the professor does not believe this, he derives a certain comfort in feeling that no one is judging his ability. For this reason, most college instructors will fight hard to prevent some committee on teaching effectiveness from visiting his classes. "I'll dismiss my class immediately if anyone walks in to judge my teaching ability," is the general comment. I have made this statement myself—but not, I hasten to add, because I am ashamed of what I am doing in the classroom or am fearful of exposing what I do to the world; rather the excuse I use, as do so many others, is that no one on such committees is knowledgeable enough in my field to judge whether or not I am doing a good job.

Then came educational television. If a professor goes on the air to teach his specialty, his department head, his dean, the university president, even members of the board of regents can tune in and see what kind of job he is doing. Even when teaching by closed circuit and not over the air, his work nevertheless can be viewed by any administrator on campus. No longer can the professor hide behind closed doors and the ignorance of his students. For this reason, most professors I know have fought educational television and have fought it hard. Generally this opposition takes the form of ridicule: "I'm no entertainer. I'm a scholar. If they want entertainment, they should get Bob Hope." Fear, cold and simple, keeps most professors off television.

In 1964, the dean at the Southwestern university where I was employed asked me to give a course by television. I agreed— out of ignorance more than anything else, for I was young and green and did not realize the professional pitfalls and the tremendous amount of work involved. After the series had been on the air and had proved mildly successful, I was approached at a departmental party by one colleague who informed me, "You and I are the only ones here with brass enough to go on television. The rest of these people are scared." However, this particular fellow never went on the tube to prove his fearlessness.

Another reason professors avoid television, beyond their reluctance to expose their knowledge of their field, is that the medium displays their classroom ability—or lack thereof.

Again, when a man goes into his classroom and shuts the door, only he and his students know his ability to teach, which is separate from his knowledge of his subject. But television allows everyone to judge his effectiveness as a lecturer. Moreover, the medium magnifies his mistakes; in person before a class the instructor occasionally can pick his teeth or scratch his dandruff without it being so noticeable, but with the camera zoomed in on just his head and the picture filling a twenty-five-inch screen those same picks and scratches assume monumental proportions.

Finally, television can have a Dr. Jekyll-Mr. Hyde effect. The professor who is mild-mannered Clark Kent in the classroom suddenly becomes Superman on the tube. He assumes visions of grandeur and thinks himself a rival to entertainers on commercial television. At my present institution, we decided to put our basic survey course in American history on television tape rather than repeat the lectures endlessly. One member of the department, who in the classroom was a fairly effective lecturer, suddenly went berserk during the taping. Blackouts, skits, costumes, even dancing go-go girls and vaudeville acts were used to present the history of the United States since 1865. When these tapes were replayed to the students, they laughed during the first two or three "lectures," but complained loudly during the remaining fifteen or sixteen shows. It is impossible to convince a professor of this type that he is not of commercial quality and that when he apes commercial television he opens himself to comparison—invariably unfavorable—with professional performers.

Because television does magnify teaching faults and because it allows many people, not just a few students, to judge a professor's competence, the medium will never be used widely in the classroom or even over the air. Professors instinctively shy away from any medium that allows a large audience to judge their competence or their teaching abilities.

DISCIPLINE IN THE CLASSROOM

It comes as a surprise to most beginning professors to discover that each class has an individual personality, just as does each person. Some classes are excellent—the students study, are prepared to discuss, and have relevant questions. Other classes are dull—the students sit there, seemingly defying you to teach them anything. A few classes are downright hostile. And also these classes vary from day to day. Sometimes when giving a lecture, even to a good class, I am aware that I am talking only to the walls; on such a day as that, I could come in with cane and straw hat to perform a little soft shoe, and no one would pay any attention. There is, occasionally, a day when the students are there in the palm of my hand, when, as I lecture, I look out and see understanding of my lecture in the eyes of the students. It is days such as this that make teaching worthwhile.

And just as class personalities vary as much as those of individuals, so also between professor and students there is the problem of who is going to be dominant. In any relationship between two people, one always is dominant (the degree of dominance varies, of course) and the other subservient. The good professor will dominate his class, while the class will dominate the poor instructor. There is no question of equality in a teaching-learning situation.

It will come as no surprise to anyone familiar with the college scene to learn that the biggest problem a professor has in dominating his class is the students who sleep through his lectures.

Of course the professor regards this as a personal insult, while the student guilty of doing this in a sense is challenging the authority of the instructor. There are several ways of handling this problem. Perhaps the best methods for stopping female students from sleeping were demonstrated to me one semester by a professor I had. When a young lady went to sleep in one of his classes, he would stop his lecture and have her awakened, saying then, "You know, Miss _____, I'm glad you went to sleep in my class; at my age, very few coeds will sleep with me." One embarrassment such as that and the young lady never slept again "with him."

On another occasion I saw this same professor stop his class when a different coed went to sleep. This one was sitting at the back of the class and had leaned her head back against the wall, there to go to sleep. His comment was, "Miss _____, I'm sorry to awaken you. You did look so nice sleeping with your mouth wide open. But you should be taking notes." Naturally she never went to sleep in that class again; no young lady wants to think she has been seen asleep with her mouth wide open.

Finally, with boys, I saw this particular professor use a different approach. He had the offending gentleman awakened and said to him, "I appreciate your going to sleep in here. These other people are watching me to see that I do my job. Some of them even would tell the president of the university if I didn't do my job. But you, by going to sleep, have demonstrated your complete confidence that I will do what I am supposed to, and thus I appreciate it." The satire involved here kept the offender awake thereafter.

Cheating, of course, is another affront to the professor who would maintain complete control over his classroom. Most of us are content to kick the offending student out of class, perhaps even to give him an F in the course. One professor I knew, his sense of humor getting the best of his intelligence, one semester came to class the day of the first examination in a particular course and told the students, "There will be no cheating in this course." Simultaneously he reached into his briefcase and pulled out a pistol, laying it on his desk very ostentatiously. Naturally the pistol was unloaded—but students complained so loudly about his bringing it to class that he was called on the dean's carpet and told never, never to repeat the joke.

One of the major methods of fighting this battle of wits to see who will dominate the classroom—students or professor—is for one student to engage in a mental battle with the professor. Perhaps it is intuition that tells a student when some particular instructor is unsure of himself; perhaps it is just some student who is insecure and wants to appear superior. But every once in a while every professor gets a student in class who tries to ask questions the professor cannot answer. This type of student will go to the library and do endless research, hunting out obscurities; then he asks questions in class not to elicit answers or to get information, but rather to "show up" the professor. I have known several college instructors actually driven from the profession by students such as this. Most of us stick with such a situation, however, gutting out the semester and hoping for better next time.

I did know a professor once who found a solution, drastic though it was, to this problem. He was teaching an American history survey course (American history to 1865) and had a student who was determined to embarrass him. Naturally in teaching a survey course, the instructor had to generalize on many points and to sweep through incidents in brief fashion. This particular student, sitting in the back of the room, carried to class every day a pocket encyclopedia of American history. He would flip through this portable reference work to find every individual, every incident mentioned by the professor. When the instructor was the slightest bit wrong, the student would speak out to call attention to the error; or when the professor was generalizing, he would point out that the incident was far more involved and would proceed to talk at some length on the subject. The professor finally decided to put a stop to this practice. Thus, on the next occasion that the student picked up an incident that had been only vaguely mentioned and elaborated at length on it, the professor announced to the class, "You know, Mr. _____ there has made me aware of something. I have been going over some of these points too hastily. Hereafter when he reminds me of not discussing one of these minor points sufficiently, I am going to ask several questions about it on the next exam. In fact, I think that the point we have just talked about will be tested in great depth on the next quiz." When he dismissed the class, he later told me, two football players were heading in the direction of the quarrelsome student. "It's funny," he said, "but that fellow hasn't asked me another question or interrupted me once since then."

There are other ways in which a student can annoy the professor, insignificant incidents in themselves but which tend to undermine discipline: by talking to a neighbor above the whisper level; by writing letters instead of taking notes; by reading a newspaper instead of listening to the lecture. Too much of this sort of thing and the professor loses control over his class.

My advice to young professors on this score is first to examine their lectures to see if they can be made more interesting and dynamic. If the professor can project an image of knowing his subject, he has less of this sort of thing with which to contend. He should examine his grading practices to see that they are fair, and he should be careful to let the students know that he genuinely wants to help them pass the course. And he should maintain a sense of humor. The ability to laugh at himself, his subject, even the entire world is absolutely necessary to the professor who would survive to retirement.

But first and foremost, the professor who is going to dominate his classes must establish his position in the first two weeks of school. In that period of time, the instructor establishes a basic level of discipline; from this he later can ease up, but he can never tighten down beyond that basic level he first establishes. Thus I come into my classes during those first two weeks just as hard and tough as I know how. I tell the students exactly what I will and will not tolerate (no talking, no reading newspapers, no sleeping). When the first one tries to do one of these things —and one of them always will test you—I fall on him like the wrath of God. When one begins to doze, I stop the class and tell him, "If you're sleepy, get out! You'll be much more comfortable in the dorm." Or "Mr. _____, if you have something to say, say it to the whole class. Otherwise, shut up!"

It is my belief that one of the few advantages of being a college professor is to have a captive audience. Thus I want no competition with my lectures (besides, all too often they can stand very little competition). However, I also believe that the professor has an obligation to dominate his class, rather than let the class dominate him, for he is hired to profess. Thus if he does not direct the lectures and the studies of the class, he is taking money under false pretenses. Which, sadly, is what many professors do.

TESTS

The making and grading of tests is the "dishwashing" aspect of teaching. It is dull dry work—which is precisely why most professors so hate it. Tests can take many forms: multiple-choice and "true-false" exams. These are very easy for students to take, and they have the supreme virtue of being very easy to grade (now there are machines that will score the things). More work for both professor and student, but far more revealing of a student's ability, is the essay examination, which requires the ability to read, think, and write. However, it has the drawback of taking a lot of time to be graded. Another type of examination is what has been called the "Take-Home Quiz"; here the professor gives the questions to the students, who take them home and have several days or weeks in which to answer the questions. Supposedly this type of examination demonstrates a student's ability to research, organize, and write. And there are specialized examinations requiring specialized knowledge: engineering assignments, laboratory quizzes in science courses (as, for example, giving the exact names of various rock specimens in geology courses), and projects in such courses as architecture, where the student is given a problem and has to make a presentation as if he was a working architect.

Some students will voice a preference for the multiple-choice examination, for there the answers are printed before him and he does not have to supply them. Other students state that they like the essay examination better, for here they can write something—anything—and make a few points whereas in the multiple-choice test the answer is right or wrong. Generally students most dislike tests—and courses—in language, mathematics, and the sciences where precise knowledge, not an approximation, is required. There is no way to fake an answer to a problem in math; either the student knows it or he does not. Thus most students prefer what have been called the "mystery disciplines," where there are no precise answers—and they can sling the bull on any given question.

Whatever the form of the examination, the professor is faced with grading the tests afterward. Particularly wretched are the essay examinations (which is why many professors avoid them), where each test may take some ten minutes to score. With fifty students in a class, it takes more than eight hours to plod through the batch. However, the mere administration of an essay exam is no guarantee that the instructor actually will spend that much time with them. Professors laughingly refer to several methods of grading such tests: throwing them down the hall, the heavier ones going farthest, and then picking up the ones nearest you, giving F's to the first ones, D's to the next ones, and so on until you get to the far end where the heaviest get A's. Or dropping the tests down a stairwell, those that are heaviest making the loudest plop when they hit and getting an A, and so on. I had a professor in ancient history who was notorious for not grading his essay tests. Apparently he took one look at the student as he entered the class and decided here was a C student, here an A student, and there an F student. He did not bother to proctor his examinations either; he wrote his questions on the blackboard and sat in the back of the room reading science fiction while the students openly copied from the textbook. One student—and I saw this—wrote one page on an examination, then sandwiched behind it some notes from a psychology course, and he received an A on the test.

Watching students approach tests is interesting. Rarely do they organize the material as they go along; instead they try the cram method. "But I stayed up all night before the quiz studying," they tell you, not realizing that this probably explains the poor grade; they were too sleepy to perform well. Freshmen approach their first examinations with the greatest confidence, however. During the first several weeks of college, they begin to assume that higher education is a snap. No one has asked them for daily papers or encouraged them to do their work; it is different from high school, where the teacher has held their hands on a day-to-day basis, patted them on the back, and encouraged them to get their little papers in. Rather, in college they can go to class if they wish, or stay in the dorm or sit in the Student Union playing cards, and no one fusses at them. "College is easy," they say—and then they take that first exam. When the papers are returned, many freshmen suffer the greatest trauma of their academic careers. For the first time in all their schooling they experience failure—an F. In the public schools, passing grades were handed out for warming a chair. In college that does not work so well. At this point, the first F, some freshmen cut and run. Others buckle down to go to work. Thus on the second and subsequent examinations they work harder.

Because of this pattern the professor faces a delicate task when he hands back the first test of the semester. He must discourage the notion of easy passing in his course, but not overly discourage the students else they will withdraw. He must strike a happy balance between fear and hope.

And because students are human—and thus inclined toward laziness—the professor has to cope with endless approaches to cheating. There is a tired old joke that periodically surfaces in academic circles about the football player (and why it must always be an athlete I don't know) who sat beside the brilliant, beautiful young lady. On every examination they made exactly

41

the same score, but when the final had been administered and the grades were posted, the young lady made an A and the football player an F. He rushed into the professor's office to demand an explanation, and was told, "You cheated." He roared back, "How do you know I cheated?" "It was easy," replied the professor. "The young lady wrote in answer to one of the questions, 'I don't know,' and you wrote, 'I don't know either.'"

There are endless methods of cheating. I do not intend a discussion of them here for fear this will become a guidebook for students. I can heartily attest, however, that the students most likely to cheat in any given situation are the public school teachers back taking courses in the summer. Their level of work almost invariably is low, their attitude defensive, and their caliber wretched. By and large they are vastly overpaid baby-sitters. Perhaps most pathetic, however, is the young female teacher who, when she graduated, wanted a "career" more than marriage and took a job in some small town. After three or four years of this, she tires of the job and begins looking around for a husband—only to discover that the few educated men in such a town (the doctor, the lawyer, and the male teachers) are already married. Thus she comes back to college in the summer, not for an education but rather to hunt a husband. She cares not a whit about the courses in which she enrolls, she does not work at them, she will cheat to get by, all the while frantically dating in search of a husband. She is indeed a pitiful type.

There is another way for students to try to pass rather than by cheating. This is to ask for a makeup test later, pretending illness, death in the family, natural calamity, anything in order to take the test later. Here the hope is that the makeup will be easier—or perhaps that the professor will give the same examination (which the student has secured a copy of) for a makeup that he gave the class. Recently a student came to my office asking for a makeup exam with the excuse that he had been ill; when I asked for a doctor's excuse from the university hospital (which students are supposed to secure when ill in order to do makeup work), he informed me he did not go to doctors inasmuch as he was a practicing Christian Scientist. Out of curiosity I asked him about Mary Baker Eddy. He answered that he had never heard of her. Of course, when tests are assigned during World Series Week, there is a spate of grandmothers dying. Just why grandmothers have such a high mortality rate is beyond me; in fact, I have had students who suffered the calamity of three grandmothers dying in one semester.

The stress on most college examinations is not the ability to reason but rather to regurgitate. The absolutely perfect student would be a tape recorder, one capable of editing the professor's lectures and giving back to him on examinations an outline of what he has said. Or a parrot that could do the same thing. Few essay questions and no multiple-choice ones require any real ability to reason. The student who can hold up a mirror to the professor on examinations and let him see his own brilliant opinions therein is all too often the A student.

Girls tend to be much better at this than boys. This observation is proved true by checking overall grade averages of boys and girls at any institution; invariably the girls will have higher grades on the average than the boys. Perhaps this is because girls are trained more at conformity and are inclined to be more passive than boys through the public school years. And girls have a better knack of mentally recording conversations (lectures); any husband can tell you that his wife can recite word for word his every word when they were courting. However, men make better graduate students than women, perhaps because the stress in graduate school is more on independent thinking, logic, and reasoning.

Most professors, when speaking candidly, will admit the failure of tests to record precisely the amount of knowledge any given student has. No test is perfect, else we all would give that type of exam. Yet they are the best yardsticks we have available to measure the amount of knowledge the student has absorbed, and thus we use them—often as a club with which to force the student to sit through our lectures, recite our opinions back to us (and thereby reinforce our belief in them), and work as hard as they do.

Because of the imperfection of tests and testing, students frequently ask the professor if he "grades on the curve." By this they mean does he assign so many A's (generally ten percent), so many B's (generally twenty percent), forty percent C's, twenty percent D's, and ten percent F's. If the professor does this, then all the students can relax and not work so hard; not so many will flunk for failure to work—and woe to the student who sets the curve too high by making exceedingly good marks. The curve method of grading was invented by educationists and was adopted by many professors who wish to hide their imperfections as teachers; no one can accuse the professor of poor teaching if his students match the national norm in their performance (grades). I heard one science professor give the perfect answer about the curve method of grading: "The only place to grade on the curve is at the swimming pool."

GRADES

One of the "inside" jokes of the teaching profession is telling of the attractive coed who comes into the professor's office at the end of the semester to say, "I'll do *anything* for an A in your course." This is a polite way of offering sex in exchange for a good grade. Perhaps I have been too naive to realize such an offer was being proffered, but I can in truth say I have never known this was happening to me; if any young lady has ever made me such a proposition, it was with such circumlocution that I was unaware of it. And in my years of teaching, I have known only one individual who claimed he had been so propositioned that I believed. He was a tall gawky graduate assistant in political science who claimed that his response was, "Anything?"

"Yes," replied the coed breathlessly, "I'll do just anything!"

"In that case," said the graduate assistant, "I recommend you get your books and go home and study."

While I have never been so approached by a coed, I have had other attempts to gain a better grade than the one actually given. On occasion my office has been awash with the tears of some young lady who wanted an A or a B. I have had interesting excuses for poor work, as has every professor. I have been told everything from a dead parent to an unwanted and unwelcome pregnancy as a reason for failure, just as I have had a few honest pilgrims who admitted poor work and asked bluntly and forthrightly for a better grade in order to qualify for graduation. I tend to look with more favor on the latter type because of the honesty factor involved.

Actually grades are an imperfect reflection of a student's ability even at their best. They are merely an approximation, the best available yardstick, for measuring the amount of work a student has done. And students rarely miss an opportunity to try to influence a professor, to compromise his objectivity. Boys do it by trying to feign interest; they imply they have read endlessly on the subject and they come to your office to discuss the topic as if it were of tremendous importance. Another way for them is to hunt out the professor's writings, plod through any available, and then casually mention how interesting they found the material.

Girls usually work the sex gimmick, not as bluntly as the young lady who says she will do "anything" for an A, but just as surely. They sit on the front row in class, staring at the professor with that wide-eyed look of breathless interest. They come to the professor's office to ask inane questions and then look at the instructor as if he were a font of knowledge. And there are many of them who wear low-cut blouses and micro-miniskirts, carelessly allowing the professor an occasional eyefull, either in the classroom or in the office. When miniskirts first appeared, I was talking with colleagues about the profusion of panties to be viewed in most classes. In some innocence, I asked if the coeds were aware of what they were doing. An old hand responded, "You're damned right they do. The way young girls are raised, they know exactly what they are showing, and when you see something it is done deliberately and for effect." He was right, of course.

Yet the professor who thinks the show is for his benefit, that the coed is infatuated with him, and tries to take advantage of it is in for trouble. One professor who was at retirement age once commented to me, "An instructor who tries to bed down one of his students is stupid. A young girl silly enough to go to bed with a professor is equally silly or stupid enough to talk about it." And the cardinal sin for professors is that old catch-all phrase "moral turpitude." Not doing it, of course, but getting caught at it. Bedding the coeds will result in firing faster than anything else.

I have listened for years to students talking about the grades they have received, and have noticed one other interesting feature on the subject. At the end of the semester, when grades are posted, students always ask each other, "What did you get?" The student who has received a good grade replied, "I *made* an A," or "I *made* a B." But for the bad grades, he will reply, "He *gave* me an F," or "He *gave* me a D." This implies, of course, that good grades are deserved but that the professor is responsible for the bad ones.

Students are human (something the cynical professor quickly learns), and thus they work only as hard as they have to in order to get by. In the course where they are forced to work, they will work. In the course where they do not have to work, they do not. Some young professors think the way to popularity with students is to give out good grades wholesale. And their classes will be filled if they do so—but with students who have only contempt for them. It has been my observation that students most admire and appreciate the professor who has standards, forces them to work, grades fairly and realistically, and tries to help the student learn as much as possible. If he sets his standards too high, with a large number of failures resulting, students avoid him; if he sets his standards too low, students sign up in large numbers but ridicule him. In the long run the professor most admired is the one who requires work and who has reasonable standards. In fact, the students in the long run will even like his subject better.

COMMITTEE WORK

Once when I was department head at a small college, I found myself serving simultaneously on seven different committees. The most onerous of these was the committee of department heads, which met weekly with the president. Nothing was ever resolved at these meetings, nothing concrete accomplished— just talk, talk, endless talk. Finally, my despair and frustration making me dangerously candid, I asked the president one day why he held these weekly sessions. His answer was equally candid: "They are good therapy for the department heads. I know they accomplish nothing, but they allow the department heads to air their gripes, feel brave in so doing, and reduce their tensions."

Such an admission of the uselessness of the committee system, except for its therapeutic value, is very rare from administrators. Nearly as rare is the professor who escapes from service on committees, for the committee is one of the most pervasive institutions on college campuses. In all my academic career I have known only one faculty member who never served on committees. He did this by playing the absent-minded professor role to the hilt; he simply "forgot" to attend committee meetings, and thus was never placed on one for that reason. I consider him one of the brightest souls I have ever encountered, for rarely have I known a committee to accomplish anything concrete; they not only are nonproductive, but generally are counterproductive. Get five or six or nine professors together—all ready to supply answers, every one of them different, to any question under the sun—and the result is protracted, endless debate (a nice word for argument).

Yet, surprisingly, there generally is at least one individual in every department who relishes committee work; who, in fact, has made his academic reputation on committee work. By taking such assignments enthusiastically when everyone else is trying desperately to avoid them, such committee-minded individuals earn their tenure, pay raises, and promotions, while simultaneously gaining a wide acquaintanceship across the campus.

The committee system is prevalent in academic communities —and will continue to be—for several reasons. Administrators like it because it lessens professional discontent harmlessly. Any professor who has a gripe, legitimate or otherwise, can be referred to a committee where his proposal will be buried under an avalanche of words, of procrastination, of debate. And should his proposal get favorable action in one committee, it can always be referred to yet another one. By the time a solution or a change is recommended, the passage of time has lessened the discontent to such an extent that no action is needed. Thus the committee becomes a means of keeping faculty discontent at a minimum.

A second reason why administrators favor the committee system is that it gives the faculty a feeling of power when in fact they have very little. Most professors want—demand—more say in how the university is run. Thus they are in part responsible for the large number of committees on the campus, although they will complain to one and all that the time they spend on these is wasted. Administrators just grin at this charge, for they know it to be true; committees are a waste of time for the most part, but they serve a psychological function of allowing the professors to feel they have power when in fact they have little or none.

Third, the committee is a marvelous means of allowing both faculty members and administrators alike to evade responsibility. Everyone knows the way to get something done is to assign the work to one competent individual. However, that individual must be willing to stick his neck out, for every positive action is subject to criticism. But when action is taken in the name of a committee, there is group responsibility—and individual anonymity. In fact, committee work reminds me of coauthoring; if you coauthor a book, you can respond graciously to a compliment on the work, but to criticism you can state that the offending section of the book was written by your coauthor. The professor can imply his own handiwork is involved in a popular decision by a committee, but to an unpopular one he can respond, "I opposed that action, but the committee overruled me."

Finally, the committee is popular because it is a handy excuse for failing to do other things. Administrators and faculty members can always cite the crush of committee assignments as a reason for failing to accomplish something. The young professor who has not written a book or even an article can say he has not had time; he is just too busy with his committee work. I have seen the committee work to advantage on this score. When some particular faculty member needed time for research, he was assigned to several committees that never met, but which then was used as an excuse to reduce his teaching load. On paper, he seemed to be doing an extraordinary amount of committee work in lieu of teaching, but in reality this was an administrative bit of sleight-of-hand to reward him with time to do research.

The one committee on most campuses that actually does some work is the one dealing with salaries and fringe benefits. Here the professor-members seem inspired, even possessed; they would make old-time labor leaders proud as they hurry to gather statistics to show how overworked and underpaid are they and their fellow professors. Inasmuch as statistics can be used to prove almost anything, this committee generally can be relied on to show that the faculty at their institution needs larger salaries, more fringe benefits, and a lighter work load, else everyone is going to decamp to move down the road to another institution; in most cases, they would find that the movement would be an exchange program, for the salary and fringe benefits at the next institution are such that the faculty there is saying it may move because of low salaries, poor fringe benefits, and high work load.

Cowardly souls that most professors are, the committee system will be with us always: a handy way to evade responsibility, diffuse discontent, and an excuse for failure to produce.

II

PROFESSIONAL ACTIVITIES

ACADEMIC CONVENTIONS

Once a year the members of most academic disciplines
gather in national convention, just as annually they also gather
in state and regional conventions. Now I am aware that the
word "convention" brings to most readers' minds thoughts of
carousing and revelry, of drinking and merrymaking. Professors are quick to respond that their meetings are not for that
purpose at all, but rather for the purpose of sharing knowledge,
of passing along recent findings within each discipline, of learning the fruits of new research. At least, this is what they state
on applications to have the state pay their way to these gatherings.

These academic conventions tend to have a universal same-
ness to them. Each schedules a number of sessions—twenty,
thirty, or forty of them. Each session supposedly is devoted to
a particular topic. On the program for that session are listed a
chairman, two or three men to read papers, and one or more

people to discuss the papers. Professors like to get on such sessions, for in many states the only way to get your way paid to a convention is to be on the program. And inasmuch as the chairman has nothing to research or write, that position is the most sought after. Next in line comes the discussant role; he also has nothing to write—and an excellent opportunity to laud his friends and damn his enemies. Then there are the slots to read papers. Young men on the rise want very much to get on every possible program, for their names get printed in the programs and they begin to make a reputation.

But very few sane men go to academic conventions to hear programs. You attend only those sessions where dear and close friends are reading. You do that in the hope that they will return the favor when you are reading, in order that neither you nor they undergo the embarrassment of reading to an empty room. I recall here a story told me by a very elderly professor of an experience that happened to him. In the 1920s, said he, the American Historical Association had not yet gone to sessions; rather it simply listed papers to be presented one after another in a specified room beginning at one in the after- noon. He was next to last on the program, but arrived at the start. As each paper was presented, a few people in the audi- ence would leave. Finally, when his turn came, only one man was left in the audience. Nevertheless he read his paper in full. Afterward he naturally hurried to thank his audience of one for remaining. "Thank me, hell," replied the individual. "I'm next, and I hope you'll return the favor by sitting through my paper."

If, in truth, academicians do not go to conventions to sit through the sessions—that is just an excuse to get the state to pay their way there—why then do they go? Because it is a boondoggle. They get to turn out their classes, escape the confines of family and community, go to some spot they otherwise could not afford to visit, and bring a little fun into normally drab lives. The publishers of textbooks invariably have cocktail parties, with free booze as the lure for listening to tales of the newest effusions from the press. And the publishers have booths at which they display their wares; at these booths the professors sign up to receive sample copies—thereby increasing their libraries (which often are deducted from federal income tax returns) at no expense. You learn the gossip of the profession—which is endless. You drink to tales of disaster to your enemies and you drink to the successes of your friends; you drink to drown the sorrow of the defeat of your friends, and you drink to drown the thought of your enemies gaining success.

And you make contacts. Contacts with publishers who might be drunk enough or foolhardy enough to sign a contract for your newest brainstorm. Contacts with potential employers who might give you a job with a higher salary and thus more prestige. So many shiny new Ph.D.'s and almost-Ph.D.'s go to the conventions looking for employment that these gatherings have been referred to many times as "the slave market." In these recent times of few jobs, those department heads who do have a vacancy to fill and are at the convention recruiting find themselves wined and dined and courted as if they were visiting royalty.

Finally the professor goes to the convention for a little forbidden fun. At a large convention city he can go to all the X-rated films he wants, even triple-X rated movies, and have some anonymity. At home he cannot go to these for he will be recognized by his students in the audience. This can be so embarrassing that most professors never catch the skin-flicks in their college town; they wait for the convention and then go.

There is a negative side to conventions, however. I once heard it stated this way: in the days before air travel made it possible to cross the country in just a few hours, most professors rarely attended a national convention and thus never saw the major men in their fields. Living in academic isolation, they easily pictured the most-published men, the authors of their textbooks and the seminal monographs and the scholarly articles, as little short of giants. Then came jet travel along with increased funds for travel, and attendance at conventions became easy. Now we meet the giants—and discover that they are tired, bald-headed, short little fellows with bad breath and fallen arches, whose talks at the banquets and luncheons are wretched. Somehow this destroys our illusions, leaves us slightly more cynical, and reminds us that we too should be working.

For people-watchers, conventions are fertile ground. Humorous yet sad is the practice of the "young-men-on-the-rise" who scurry about the hotel corridors and the lobby looking to buttonhole the grand old men. Desperately they want to make an impression, to become known by the major figures within their discipline. They hope to gain status by being seen with some important man. And there is the possibility that the well-known scholar might be persuaded to write an introduction for the young man's next book or that somehow he might be influenced to write a favorable dust-jacket blurb. The sad part is that when one of these young-men-on-the-rise corners a well-known figure, he never looks the older man in the eye; instead his own eyes constantly are searching the crowd, looking for someone even better known whom he can buttonhole.

And among young men in the profession, there is a belief that at the convention the giants of the discipline are somewhere in the proverbial smoke-filled room making major decisions. They think if they can just catch one of these old men, he might invite the young scholar back to join the inner circle. That is the young man's major goal: to be invited to join the greats back in the smoke-filled room. I know one professor who is fairly successful, but who stays resoundingly drunk at every convention he attends out of frustration that he is not among the select few off somewhere making big decisions. Actually there is no smoke-filled room at the convention. The old men are not visible in the hotel lobby or corridors because they tire easily and thus stay in their rooms in order to rest; or they stay there because they have long since learned that the sessions are not worth attending; and they stay there to avoid being buttonholed by young clawing scholars who talk endlessly.

Thus fortified with the gossip of the profession, the booze of the publisher, the names of leading scholars to be dropped, and possibly the hope of a better job, the professor returns to his institution talking about how marvelous were the papers, how high the intellectual tone of the convention, and how much his institution gained by having him there to represent it. Because he wants his way paid to next year's gathering, he is careful upon his return to write the program chariman for that convention suggesting yet another "seminal" paper which he, the professor, stands ready to read for the enlightenment of his brethren. Thus the position of program chairman contains real power, inasmuch as it carries with it the authority to put people on the program, thereby incurring an obligation for them to do likewise for you at some subsequent date.

WRITING

"Publish or perish" has been a catch-slogan of the academic world for a dozen and more years now, although it is not heard as much recently as previously. If the slogan was true, however, most professors would soon perish. I saw figures several years ago, published by the Department of Health, Education, and Welfare (one of those federally subsidized research projects of benefit only to the grant recipient) which indicated that seventy-five percent of all Ph.D.'s never publish anything beyond that contained in their dissertations—if they publish anything from that. This means that only twenty-five percent try to research and write, once out of graduate school. And I assure you that the remaining three-fourths of them do not perish! Look in any university, and their name is professor.

Still, the one-quarter that remains is sufficient to innundate the world in an ocean of words, of articles, books, monographs, pamphlets, reports. From the moment a student enters graduate school, he is made aware of the status associated with publication. Simultaneously he is placed in seminars where he has to write learned papers (too often associated with research the professor currently is doing and from which he intends to publish). He is given an introductory course in the discipline, in which he is taught the tribal secrets of collecting evidence, doing research, drafting the paper, and larding it with the paraphernalia of scholarship—*i.e.*, footnotes and bibliography.

The major fault of this system is that the professors conducting the seminars cannot themselves write. Thus everyone, student and professor, falls back on the safety of writing like all other scholars in that particular field: fact and footnote, fact and footnote—dry as dust, all adjectives and adverbs squeezed out —and with a heavy reliance on "academic" words of Latin and

57

Greek extraction. Three pages of the printed result are equal to one sleeping tablet. Try to think of someone you know, with the exception of students who cannot avoid the painful exercise, who actually reads a history textbook, a tome on political science, a work on anthropology or any of the other -ologies.

And because most professors cannot write graceful, readable, literary prose, God help the poor scholar who does. The most certain way to become suspect within the academic community is to write a book that sells other than to the captive market of students. Let the public buy and read your work and you are accused of that most heinous of crimes—being a popularizer. The logic involved is flawless. Says the author of a standard (nonselling) tome: "My work is good and did not sell. Yours sells. Therefore it cannot be any good." That such an attitude is prevalent is easily determined. Yet to suggest that such an attitude is unscholarly is considered heresy. However, the only reason for writing is the assumption that someone is going to read that which is penned; in short, the goal of writing is to communicate. Somehow in the scholarly world, however, status is in inverse proportion to the number of readers. Inasmuch as few people read scholarly writing, the reality has been made a virtue, and the fewer readers a man has the more scholarly his writing must be.

Therefore scholars have become mere legmen for journalists and novelists, people who are trained in a skillful and literate use of words. The failing there is that journalists and novelists all too frequently do not let the truth stand in the way of a good story. Thus on the one hand you have scholars with the facts and on the other people who can write but who do not have a reverence for the truth and proper rules of evidence. And God help the poor professor who tries to combine both good research and good writing. Yet, ironically, when you ask a professor to name the best-known scholar in his field, the top man or men, he almost invariably will name someone who can do both!

The moral here is obvious: young scholar, do not research and write well unless you make it big. Then you are all right, but until you reach the top you are merely prostituting your training. Walter Prescott Webb, a giant in the field of Western American history, once commented about this aspect of the scholarly world to me: "When you publish, never expect understanding and appreciation from the people you most normally would expect it from, your own colleagues. They will make fun of your efforts, carry tales about you, belittle you. This they did to me—until I became president of the American History Association. Then they were glad to drop my name."

Most professors who publish begin at the "article" level. By this, I mean they try to write a short paper for publication in a learned journal of their discipline. And there is a definite "pecking order" to these journals. At the bottom, carrying least prestige, are the local ones. Sometimes these are but mimeographed-and-stapled pamphlets carrying three or four such effusions. In the middle are the regional journals, and at the top are the learned quarterlies of the major national associations. There even are efforts to stratify these journals beyond the simple distinction of breadth of geographic scope; one way is to differentiate between those journals having a "Board of Editors" and those that do not. The implication is that those with a Board of Editors submit their articles, previous to publication, to the editorial consultants for an evaluation as to the worth of the article. I have worked in an editorial capacity on a regional journal and presently am an editorial consultant to three others (one national, two regional), and only once have I been asked to read an article previous to its publication to rule on its merits. When I did work as an assistant editor on a quarterly, we used our "editorial consultants" only as a cover for those articles we rejected; "We regret to inform you that our editorial consultants do not feel your article merits publication . . .," was our reply—when, in truth, never once did we consult them.

When writing such articles, academicians tend to worry excessively that "someone will discover something wrong in it." This fear of making an error has caused friends of mine to work continuously on one article for one, two, and even three years before submitting it for publication. I have never understood this fear, for I truthfully believe no one actually reads journal articles. I have published more than thirty of the things, and I have yet to receive a letter questioning some fact I have used in one. I have occasionally received a query about where information on the subject might be found from some poor soul writing a similar article, and a few friends have written to say they saw the effort and to congratulate me on its publication. However, even my friends, under questioning, reply that they did not bother to read the article in question. Perhaps this nonreading of articles does not apply in the sciences, but I know in my own and related disciplines (the liberal arts) this is true. No one reads the damn things! They are too busy writing their own articles to read those written by someone else. If there are any readers out there, it has to be poor captive graduate students—or insomniacs.

After the articles, in theory, comes the book. The good scholar investigates some topic, deriving therefrom several articles, and then he writes the monograph. Most academicians produce their books on what professional writers would call speculation—that is, without a contract in hand prior to the writing. Once the manuscript is completed, then the scholar begins to think of what press he will dignify by allowing it to publish such a fine and scholarly work. To my great astonishment I have found that few professors have the slightest idea how to make contact with publishing houses. Most of them begin, naturally, by sending the manuscript to a New York house without a letter of inquiry. The manuscript simply is delivered by the postman—what I have heard referred to as "transom books," inasmuch as they are dropped on publishers' desks almost literally through the transom. Many of the houses have quit reading transom books because the return is too small on the few books that are accepted this way from the many that arrive. Too many readers have to be employed to sort out the trash.

Two other methods of reaching publishers are open to professors with ready manuscript. One is the college traveler—a nice name for traveling salesmen employed by the major publishers of textbooks. The other is the convention, at which there always are a few editors present. Sadly, however, most academicians could not sell a gold dollar for ninety cents—or as an earthy colleague once said, "Most profs couldn't make out in a two-bit whorehouse with a twenty-dollar bill in their pockets."

The conversation of professors trying to sell a manuscript (even occasionally an idea for a manuscript) to the publisher or to the college traveler reveals the incredible naiveté of the entire tribe. "But this book is needed," they say with strong stress on the word *need*. "It will fill a gap in scholarship." The truth, as every editor knows, is that no book is needed if it will not pay its own freight; comes the meeting of the stockholders, and the editor who talks about filling gaps in knowledge and publishing books that are needed will quickly find himself among the unemployed. I should mention that most New York houses do publish a number of books each year that they know will not sell—books that have something to say that needs saying. Generally these are intended as prestige items. My point is that most major publishers have more of a social conscience than the public—and professors—give them credit for.

The academician who wants to place a manuscript or ink a contract to write a book should lift a few pages from salesmen's handbooks. I have found in negotiating contracts that the author must exude confidence. All he has to sell is himself, his ability to stand and deliver a manuscript, and the thought that the work will have a market. The prospective professorial author will find a far more receptive ear for his idea when he talks about potential market than when he discusses the need for his work. Selling books to the public is a hard task; in fact, many of them are bought on whim and spur-of-the-moment decisions. No editor knows what will be faddish or stylish or a momentary sensation a year, two years, or even three years hence. Thus he works on a blend of experience, hope, intuition, and luck. To persuade him that a manuscript is needed is very difficult; to convince him that the final product will sell is much easier. The best sales pitch, the one most likely to secure a contract, however, is that which stresses both items. No editor likes to think of himself as a crass businessman pandering to public whim; he would prefer to dwell on the self-image of a moulder of public opinion, an uplifter of the level of culture, and a contributor to the social fabric of the nation—while simultaneously satisfying his stockholders. Thus the professor should stress first that his book will make both himself and the publisher rich, while simultaneously filling a need and extending the frontiers of knowledge—in exactly that order.

The professor who successfully manages to sell his product and gets his book published is not going to receive the applause of his colleagues, however. If the tome falls dead from the press and is never read (and I would repeat here what I said earlier about articles: other professors do not read them), he can console himself that it was scholarly. But the gravest sin a professor can make is to publish too much. If he turns out a book a year, he must be doing hasty research. And God help the poor fool who both publishes much and is widely read by the public—until he gains a national reputation. Until he achieves sufficient prominence to have his name "dropped," he goes through great agony. I once had the head of a department where I was applying for a job tell me he could not hire me because I had published more than his entire staff put together; "It would just make everyone mad," he informed me.

I suspect that every author who writes with any facility, and thus turns out a lot of words, occasionally has fears that his creativity is drying up—that he has gone to the well once too often. Especially is this fear felt when he is facing some imminent deadline and has very little copy ready. Writing comes easiest when an author is not self-conscious. When I was in graduate school, one of my professors informed me that every sentence I wrote ought to be rewritten (before proceeding to the next sentence) until the words were as chiseled in marble; needless to say, that particular professor had written very little. Writing comes easiest when the author is not self-conscious. When he begins to believe that he is composing for the ages, that three or four hundred years hence people will be reading his books, that he is achieving immortality through his literary creation, then he becomes self-conscious and thereby destroys the very thing that enabled him to write easily—which is not taking himself too seriously. And most scholars do take them-selves seriously!

If I were giving advice to the young professor about to em-bark on an academic career, I would suggest as a safe goal an article a year and a book every five years. This is sufficient to satisfy the head of his department and his dean, but not so much as to threaten his colleagues unduly.

Finally, there are those professors who choose not to publish at all. In fact, a majority of them do not. And they have a ready defense mechanism. "I just want to be a good teacher," they smugly say, implying that a scholar cannot be good in the class-room and still find time to research and write. I have observed that, with but rare exception, the producing scholar is also the best lecturer. Without *any* exception the professor who would do well in the classroom must continue to research. Advance-ments in every discipline make it necessary for the professor to research constantly, else he will become hopelessly outdated. Not all research results in publication; there are nonpublishing scholars who research regularly. But they are very rare. It may be personal bias to say so, but I tend to believe that the professor who states that he does not write so that he can concentrate on good teaching probably is not doing either.

THE BOOK REVIEW

Because of the increase in the number of publishers and of academicians under pressure to spew out books, there is an annual effusion of literally thousands of tomes—which, in turn, are sent to the ever-increasing number of academic journals for review. Thus a regular part of the professor's work is writing reviews of books for one or another of the learned journals in his field. In fact, without these book reviews, most professors would become even more helplessly out-of-date in their own fields. The professor is busy teaching, researching, writing, playing golf, or downtown working at a second job, and he has little time—perhaps I should say inclination—to read in his own field. This, at least, is what we say publicly. The truth is that we are little inclined to read books in our own disciplines because most of them are deadly dull. Besides, it is physically impossible to read all the books issued in just our own narrow field of specialization. Thus of necessity we have to rely on book reviews. We all therefore are benefactors of the book review—and some of us are its victims.

In theory the reviewer of each book is a specialist in the field under review. Ideally the editor of each journal picks only a man who has published in the same area to review a new book. Forty or fifty years ago this practice worked pretty well. There were only four or five journals, and it was easy to find four or five competent scholars in similar or closely related fields to review the new work. Now, however, there are journals by the score. In my own field of Western American history, there is at least one journal in each state, along with several regional and national quarterlies devoted to the subject. Thus when a book in Western American history appears, it will be reviewed by some twenty-five to thirty journals. Obviously there are not that many specialists who have actually published in any given area. Thus the good men, the ones who have published in that specialty, review the book for the national or regional journals (or for the state journals whose book-review editors work very fast and secure a commitment early from one of the good men). The remainder of the book-review editors have to settle for lesser men to do the work.

Having worked on a journal, I have seen this process of selecting reviewers at first hand. And I know it even better from
talking with other editors. Generally the editor gets around to
the new crop of books once every three months. He then stacks
up everything that has arrived and makes his cut. Into one stack
go the books he personally considers unfit for reviewing; a journal does get about two books for every one it reviews. However,
these books that are not sent out for review are not wasted—
they go into the journal editor's personal library.

A second category of books are those the editor considers only
marginally worth reviewing. These he handles one of several
ways. Perhaps the most-often employed is to write a fifty- to
seventy-five-word review of each of these for inclusion in the
journal after the regular-length reviews. And again these books
then go into his personal library. Another method of handling
these is to lump four or five of the marginal books together and
assign them to a reviewer, who agrees to write one review of
only regular length about all five.

The third category of books is those the editor believes to be
of considerable worth to the area of specialty of his journal. And
finally there are the fine-press books, those whose deluxe print-
ing, binding, and graphics make them sell for $25 to $50. This
last category of books the editor sends to close friends, or else
to big names in the field whom he wishes to court. But it is the
third category of books that consumes most of his time. And
here the editor exercises his prejudices, rewards his friends,
massages his own ego, and throws excrement on his own and his
friends' enemies.

If the book under consideration is by a major figure in the
field, the editor generally tries to choose another major figure
to review it. When it happens that he is too late to secure the

man he wants for the review, he then falls back on friends or people he wants to have for friends. When the book under consideration is by someone the editor dislikes (or who may have written an unfavorable review of one of his friends' books), the editor can deliberately choose someone who will cut the book badly. Or he can select an unknown graduate student to do the review, which in itself is an insult; the implication, by inference, is that the book is unworthy of review by a serious scholar.

And there are in the profession, every field of it, book reviewers who have made their reputation only by writing cutting reviews. These are people who generally have never written a book, but who are known for their facile wit, barbed comments, and general disdain for every published work. In some circles, the scholar has not arrived who has not been slashed by one of these professional cutters. The editor who chooses one of these types to review a book knows he is giving the book a "thumbs down" evaluation. Another way of insuring the same thing is to send a book to a young-man-on-the-rise, one who intends to make it to the top over dead bodies; invariably this type will wield the meat ax.

Also in the profession, every field of it, are scholars who never give an unkind review. If they cannot find something good to say about a book, they give it an innocuous review (merely summarize content without comment or evaluation). For the editor to send a book to such a scholar is to insure a favorable or at least innocuous review.

Thus the editor wends his way through the stack of books at hand, chuckling at knifing his enemies, self-pleased at helping his friends, hopeful of making new ones, incurring obligations and paying off old scores. His next step is to write a letter to each potential reviewer, asking will he or will he not review the stated book and giving a deadline and desired length of review.

The scholar receives the invitation and must make his own decision. Sometimes this is a pleasant task. If the work is by a friend or by someone he wishes to have for a friend (or at least under obligation to him), he accepts with the intent of writing a good review. If the work is by an enemy or by someone who has cut one of the would-be reviewer's friends, he accepts with glee, intending to write so dreadful a review as to end forever the author's pretensions. And if the book is in competition with the reviewer's own works or reaches opposite conclusions from what the reviewer previously has reached in print, then he accepts happily, intending to lacerate the author for his factual inaccuracies, his lack of depth, his shoddy writing, his outdated maps, and his poor choice of graphics. Finally, if the author of the work is unknown to the would-be reviewer and the work no competition, he accepts or rejects the invitation at his own discretion.

The editor receives the returns, sending the books along to those who accept and going through the same process previously mentioned to secure reviewers for those books not accepted. Thus, finally, books are placed for review.

In order to evaluate a book in scholarly fashion, the reviewer obviously should read the book first. Not to do so is dishonest (*i.e.*, unscholarly). Yet every author has read reviews of his work that obviously were written by a reviewer who had read only the dust jacket and possibly the Introduction and Conclusion. Publishers are aware of this laziness on the part of many reviewers, which is why most book jacket blurbs read like a favorable review. Following cardinal rule number one (to read the book) is the second rule: that the reviewer ought to understand the book. Such also is not always the case. Many a good book has received an unkind evaluation from a reviewer who obviously missed the point of the entire work.

Once the book is read—and understood—the reviewer then has an obligation to accomplish, as I see it, three things in his critique. First, he should summarize the content. This performs the vital function of allowing other scholars to know the contents without having to read the book; a vital function of reviews, as stated earlier, is to allow the scholar to keep abreast of his field even though he cannot read everything that is printed. And there is a trick or two to be remembered by the reviewer in summarizing content. He should slant the summary of content to his readership. Thus if he is reviewing a book about the entire Southwest, the review to appear in the *New Mexico Historical Review*, he should briefly summarize the entire book, then concentrate the bulk of his space on that part of the book specifically of concern to New Mexicans.

Second, the reviewer should tell the author's purpose and assess how well the author accomplished this. Most writers state in the Preface or Introduction exactly what it is they intend to do in the book, although occasionally they omit this information and it has to be surmised from the content of the book itself. An author can be judged only in the light of what he set out to accomplish and how well he accomplished it. If his purpose is merely to rescue from oblivion some deserving figure by relating the man's biography, or to chronicle some overlooked event, then that is his purpose and he should be judged on how well he shows why the man or event should be better known. If, on the other hand, he is grasping after some larger purpose, that should be the scale on which he is weighed. This second point seems obvious, but apparently it is not—scholars have a strong tendency not to review the book at hand or not to evaluate the author for what he set out to do; rather they all too often choose to review the book they feel the author *ought to have written.* I heard a friend once say, regarding potential reviews of his latest book, that his fervent wish was that they review the book he had written rather than the book they wanted him to write. Reviews of this type castigate the author for his sins of omission rather than for any sins of commission. Recently a reviewer of one of my books gave a point by point summary of my effort, pausing after capsulizing each section to point out what opportunities I had missed to enlarge upon the failures of humanity and to advance the liberal political philosophy thereby.

Finally, the writer of any scholarly review has the obligation to state his conclusions as to whether the book was worth doing, that is, to evaluate the worth of the author's purpose. Many a book I have seen was not worth the time, expense, and effort to bring it into print; the trees would better have been left in the forest rather than been chopped down to make paper for the book. Curiously, however, it is here—the most scholarly part of a review and the point where the reviewer has an opportunity, nay rather an obligation, to put the work in proper scholarly perspective—that academic reviewers most often fail. Perhaps this is because in reaching such a conclusion the reviewer also is exposing his critical faculties to public gaze. And at heart all academicians are cowards.

Instead of assessing a book on its merits (that is, what the author's purpose was, how well he accomplished it, and was it worth accomplishing), most reviewers who want to fault a work do so on minor points. I have read numerous reviews of books on Latin American history, for example, where a reviewer makes the author seem a cousin of Atilla the Hun because he omitted a few accent marks on Spanish words. Another such device is to hunt assiduously through the book for typographical errors, holding each up to light of public ridicule as if it were a deadly scholarly sin. Most prevalent of all, however, is to search out the minor errors of fact—and enumerate each in dreary detail. The truth is, every book published has a few typographical errors, and every book published has a few factual errors. God knows the author of each can find them in his own works. Thus my point: *every book published can be reviewed unfavorably if the reviewer wishes to cut it.*

Of course, there are ways and then there are ways of demolishing a book the reviewer does not like. He can use a small pen knife, damning with faint praise. He can use a Bowie knife and carve out small portions, yet leave a living carcass behind. Or he can choose a rapier and puncture with many small wounds. Or a broadsword and leave slashing and bleeding cuts. Or the meat ax and simply pound a work to death. The last named method can, on occasion, backfire. For example, in 1931, Walter Prescott Webb published *The Great Plains,* in which he offered new and refreshing insights into the pattern of settlement of Mid-America. Professor Fred A. Shannon reviewed this book in the *American Historical Review* with the meat ax. Webb later asserted that had his work received a mildly critical or even mildly favorable review it would have died of inattention, yet because it was attacked so roundly people read it, it became a classic work of interpretation, and thereby Webb secured his reputation as one of the three or four top historians of this century. It does take a certain amount of courage for a reviewer to attack a book so sharply, however; and, as I have said previously, most professors are cowards.

71

Other sidelights of the book-reviewing business that occur to me and that give insights into the scholarly world include some curious things. For example, rarely is a scholarly book reviewed harshly in the academic quarterlies if first it has received good reviews in the *New York Times Book Review* or in the major Chicago and Los Angeles newspapers. If *Saturday Review* or even *Time* and *Newsweek* give their imprimatur to a book, the scholarly community tends to agree. Nor will many scholars cut a book that is handsome in format or high in price. "Pretty" books tend to get good reviews. These factors show that scholars are influenced far more than they will admit by "popular" evaluations and by physical format and price.

Turning to reviews that are not slashing in approach, those written favorably, again we find that few reviewers have the courage to give unvarnished praise to any book. Always they find a few faults: several paragraphs of praise are followed by a short notation of the shortcomings of the work—and then by a summary that begins, "Despite these flaws, Professor Blank's work is of value. . . ." This tendency to find a few redeeming features in the worst of books and a few faults in the most praiseworthy effort stems from two sources: first, few professors have the courage of absolute conviction; therein lies the secret of survival in the academic world. And, second, the academician who fails to find some flaws in the best of works is admitting his own inferiority; he has to find something wrong in order to demonstrate that he is smarter than the author of the book he is reviewing.

For several years now I have been teaching a course in how to write history. I am not innovative enough to have dreamed up this approach; rather I had such a course in college, liked the idea, and persuaded my department head here to allow me to offer it. In it I tell budding scholars (a nice way of saying gradu-ate students trying to become professors) never to review a book unless they can find something good to say about it. If the work is totally without value, I tell them not to lie but rather to return the book to the editor so someone else can review it. The reason for this is one of survival; if you cut a book, the author and his friends will cut yours when you publish. This rule was given to me in graduate school, and every time I have violated it I have subsequently regretted it. Of course, if you never intend to write a book, you can violate this rule endlessly, for the author you cut, and his friends, will never have a chance to strike back.

The man who taught me this rule himself violated it on occa-sion. Once, for example, he was sent a book for review with a deadline some three months away. Inasmuch as the author was a well-known authority in his field, my professor thought it would be a good one and set it back on the shelf to await a convenient time to write the review. A week before his dead-line he pulled it down only to discover to his horror that the authority had goofed on the book. It was wretched. My profes-sor was caught; he could not return the book to the journal that had sent it to him, for too much time had elapsed, nor could he in honesty review it favorably. He wrote a cutting review—and suffered a similar fate on his next book at the hands of the author and his friends.

The review completed, it is returned to the editor of the journal, who then demonstrates his superiority over the re-viewer by "editing" it. I use quotes here because few—very few —editors of academic quarterlies have the background in gram-mar to know what the true function of an editor is. Most work from intuition here. And a few editors are so egotistical—or so cowardly—that they rewrite the entire review to suit what they feel their readership (should I say the editorial board within the university that publishes the journal?) wants, leaving the author no style of his own.

Then comes the process of selection for reviews to include in a particular journal. In placing the reviews to be printed, the editor almost invariably will select the best-known reviewer's efforts to position first and (curiously) last among the reviews in a given issue. Failing to have a big-name reviewer, the editor will place first and last the books written by the best-known scholars. He also will try to mix his reviews: a good one, an innocuous one, a vicious one, so that no two similar ones are in close proximity.

And most editors, inasmuch as the majority of them do not themselves write books, take a perverse delight in publishing reviews that cut hard. To do so, they will tell you, titillates their readership, stirs controversy, and increases circulation; some will even claim that it advances the cause of scholarship, for it makes authors more careful. Closer to the truth is the fact that strongly worded, unfavorable reviews massage these editors' egos for not having written themselves, and probably deep down they hope that cutting reviews will discourage others from writing.

Here then is the book-review system of the academic world. The book review is intended to help scholars keep abreast at a time of great publication; so much is being published that the scholar cannot read everything, and reviews tell him what is worth his time and what is not. They are supposed to assess the contribution each author makes to his discipline. The book review also, in theory, aids the reviewer in keeping abreast of his own field, sharpens his critical sense, makes him a better author himself, and allows him to perform a service for his fellow scholars.

But the book review, in all its present glory, more often than not is an assessment of who are each editor's friends and enemies, who are each reviewer's friends and enemies, a sad commentary on the lack of courage among scholars and a wide advertisement of the absence of scholarship among scholars. It demonstrates how human are the "experts" that assign and write reviews, and it raises the old question of "who judges the judges." Very few of these reviews actually accomplish what a good book review should do: summarize content, tell the author's stated or unstated purpose, inform the reader how well that purpose was accomplished, and assess the contribution of the book to the advancement of truth.

THE AFTER-DINNER SPEECH

Professors find the after-dinner speech a ubiquitous part of their lives, both at the giving and receiving ends. As "experts" (which I have heard defined as "someone from more than fifty miles out of town and carrying a briefcase") they frequently are asked to speak to local service clubs and special interest groups. Here the college instructor is caught in a neat dilemma: he wants the public recognition that giving talks will bring him and he hates the bother and inconvenience; yet at the same time he is fearful of exposing his ignorance to public view and he knows he will not get paid for his effort.

The businessmen who usually are in charge of service clubs take a very socialistic attitude about asking university professors to speak to them: they expect the service for nothing. These same businessmen will think nothing about forking up fifty or one hundred dollars for a speaker represented by one of the bureaus that specialize in furnishing "programs" for such organizations (and there are such animals—businesses that make their money from supplying programs for service clubs, school assemblies, you name it; they supply a speaker). Often these businessmen will pay one hundred dollars to see some world traveler show films he made in India in 1940, but not a nickel to a university professor. He is paid by the public and should do this extra work for nothing. As a reward he gets a certificate of appreciation. I could paper the walls of my house with copies of the Optimist's Creed, the Rotarian's Pledge, and the Kiwani's certificate of appreciation; I could knock all my enemies on the head with the gavels I have been given, and I can call my children to dinner with gift bells. But I cannot buy groceries with these. In fact, I do not recall ever being given money to pay for the gas these trips cost me. All I have received for each, beyond a certificate of appreciation, is a dinner that too often defies digestion. It is little wonder, then, that I and other professors repay service club members in kind: we give them a speech that defies digestion. The wonder is that we continue to be asked to speak to such groups.

And professors constitute an audience for endless and assorted banquets and luncheons, at which we have to listen to such speeches. Professors are not the only Americans to suffer this abomination; almost all citizens of this country with any pretensions of "culture" suffer this same malady. Perhaps it is the Puritan ethos that makes us think we must dignify every solemn occasion with pompous oratory. I refer to the Puritan ethos because the after-dinner speech is the American way of ritual suffering.

The ritual is a legacy to us from the pre-television, pre-radio, and pre-movie age. In that earlier time the only way rural and isolated communities of people kept current with ideas and changes, or simply absorbed interesting information, was by reading magazines and books—and by means of the Chautauqua (or lecture) circuit. Ralph Waldo Emerson, David Thoreau, and a host of other so-called intellectuals made a comfortable living in that age by riding the lecture circuit. Bad speaking was tolerated, even enjoyed, then because it was the most intellectually stimulating event for weeks. This holdover from an earlier age is responsible for more suffering—and probably indigestion—than any other aspect of the American past.

The entire after-dinner-speech system has become a ritual, almost as sacred and as rigid as a high mass. During the meal there is considerable levity, gossiping, even selling (making "contacts" is the current phrase describing this aspect). The meal itself is of little consequence, as restaurateurs catering to this type of business well know; speakers who make such circuits regularly refer to the meals collectively as "rubber chicken." And chicken it frequently is, chicken with about as much personality as a toilet lid—or ham or turkey or some other unidentifiable mess. The more pretensions the group has to culture, the more unidentifiable the menu will be.

After the meal is mercifully concluded, the master of ceremonies takes charge. He generally is a fellow of little wit and less intelligence, else he would realize what a spectacle he is making of himself. He introduces the exalted guests and the venerated types at the head table, and then presents the man responsible for the speaker of the day. The introducer often will begin by suggesting that the audience move its chairs around to get a better view of the proceedings to follow. There follows the scraping of chairs, a last bit of talk and laughter, and a settling down seeking comfort in which to go to sleep. The audience is stuffed. All their blood is at their stomachs, and thus they are at their worst intellectually to hear something serious.

The introducer provides a flowery introduction of a man "who needs no introduction," listing honors, degrees, and writings that make the speaker seem a fountain of learning, wisdom, and intelligence. Polite applause follows, whereupon the speaker at this point is under great pressure to produce the ritual joke. "In the valley of the blind, a one-eyed man would be king," once wrote H. G. Wells; in the after-dinner speech setting, even the feeblest jest evokes a belly laugh. There is something almost obscene about the ritual joke. At this solemn gathering, it is out of place, and the audience responds like small children snickering at something a teacher has innocently said that has a double meaning. The ritual joke is as out of place as the sound of someone passing gas in church.

The ritual has now progressed to the point of the speech itself. The speaker launches into his talk, the words rolling out in sonorous, pasted-together phrases so familiar to the orator. It drips words of Greek and Latin extraction, and it reeks of artificial alliteration, a literary device that often passes for "pretty writing." The speaker fills his paragraphs with buts, whereases, yets, and therefores. And the audience tunes out, sits glassy eyed in stony silence throughout, hearing little and caring less. People slump in their chairs so they can sleep without falling to the floor, just as they do in church when the minister begins his sermon. Many such speakers have a remarkable ability to turn a sentence into two paragraphs and to make ten minutes seem like two hours. But when he finishes at last, there is ritual applause, a polite way to awaken that part of the audience fortunate enough to be asleep—and then there is a ritual line of

78

listeners from the audience (including some of those who have been sleeping) who come forward to shake the speaker's hand and tell him how much they enjoyed his talk.

Ritual suffering—we do not feel we have been at an inspirational or educational or intellectual meeting unless we have suffered. The truth is that today most of us are exposed to new ideas and to material of an educational nature by television and the movies—and by professional entertainers and professional speakers. Therefore the ideal after-dinner speech would be to clear away the platform, lower a screen, and show a film. The after-dinner speaker of today, especially amateur ones such as college professors, cannot compete with the polished performers of television; they are bound to suffer by comparison. The television special of an educational nature almost invariably uses the voices, if not the on-camera narration, of a professional actor; I can recall very few that employed the pedant responsible for the text or the ideas that motivated the show.

The genuinely good orators of our day—and there are more of them now than ever before—are those who poke fun at pomposity, who use wit and wisdom in equal measure, and who speak in a nonpublic oratorical voice. Thereby they entertain us at the level we really most appreciate. This explains why a Will Rogers was so popular—and he generally has more genuine wisdom in his speeches than most after-dinner speakers who roll Latinized phrases with such ease.

III

PROFESSIONAL ATTITUDES

THE TENDENCY TO ANARCHY

Because professors, however erroneously, see themselves as individualists and because each one thinks he has the answers to all the world's problems, there is a strong tendency in the academic community toward anarchy. Every professor, however lowly his rank, feels he knows how to drive the wagon and should be given the reins, that he should be president of the university; as with Napoleon's corporal, each has a marshal's baton in his mental knapsack. In the name of this individuality, professors always pay lip-service to the concept of democracy —*i.e.*, they want to be allowed to vote on everything. And they gripe endlessly about the directives they receive from those in authority over them.

Historically in academic communities, scholars have had the right to vote on certain aspects of their work: courses, requirements for degrees, and other such academic-related items. This tradition dates from medieval times when universities first were organized. However, in the United States, those employed to administer the colleges traditionally have enjoyed the obligation to make decisions about pay and promotion. Now the cry is on to allow the professors to vote on these matters. Yet mediocre types—and that includes at least three-quarters of the academic community—always vote for mediocrity, making that commodity cancerous in its growth. A sound rule of thumb in the academic world is never to bring anything to a vote if it involves quality! Voting on promotion will bring on an orgy of mutual back-scratching by people unworthy of promotion, while voting on pay raises always results in lock-step increases in salary. And without merit increases being highly visible, there will be little merit displayed—despite all professorial talk of antimaterialism.

For example, the head of a political science department told me about his one effort to allow democracy when the question of pay raises arose. He called a departmental meeting and announced how much money he had been given for the following year's pay raises and asked the department to vote on the issue. Naturally all voted for an equal amount to be given to each member of the department. Then, according to the department head, there was a sly procession of supplicants coming individually to his office to tell him why each felt he deserved more than the others. All paid lip-service to the concept that all were equal but, in the words of George Orwell's *1984*, each secretly felt a little more equal than the rest.

To hide their feelings of inadequacy, college professors will state that they believe in merit raises, but they insist that "merit" is impossible to define with precision. "Yes, we believe in it," they say, "but who among us is capable of judging merit?" Large enrollments in particular professors' classes can be explained away on the score of "easy grades" or else content (some subjects simply are more popular than others). Publication likewise cannot be counted as meritorious, according to these Philistines, because one cannot weigh quality with a scale or apply the timeclock to excellence—the nonpublished claims to be gestating a seminal work. When asked why not rely on student evaluations, the nonmeritorious reply that the professor who is extraordinarily easy will receive extraordinarily high markings. It is my belief, however, that student evaluations are of great value, but on a three- to five-year basis. Over the longer period of time the judgment of students tends to be pretty fair. And enrollment is a valuable yardstick of teaching effectiveness; over the years the teacher who is dull, who is dry, who is unfair in his grading gains a reputation for such, just as the teacher who is good, who is fair, and who is enjoyable gets a different reputation.

The rallying cry of academic anarchists is the slogan "academic freedom," a term much abused. Perhaps more sins of irresponsibility have been hidden behind the slogan of academic freedom than any other in the professorial world. But freedom always brings responsibility, be it academic, social, political, cultural, or economic. "Tenure" is the other facade of protection behind which the academic incompetent and the academic anarchist hide. Tenure means simply that a man cannot be fired except for cause; generally "cause" translates as moral turpitude. Short of playing around with the coeds, a professor cannot be fired no matter how wretched he is as a lecturer, how lazy he is, or how little he publishes. I have observed that almost invariably the first people to raise the cry of academic freedom and of tenure are those that should be fired first.

And in every case with which I am familiar where the American Association of University Professors (a trade union for liberal, militant, and/or incompetent professors) has investigated a university and has blacklisted it for violation of tenure or academic freedom, the university has been dead right in firing the individual under question. Strangely, however, those individuals fired and who cry violation of tenure or violation of academic freedom generally wind up getting a good job in some liberal Eastern or West Coast school.

Griping about the boss is a widespread human failing not confined to the academic community. However, professors have raised this trait to a fine art. The easiest way for a newly hired instructor to gain acceptance by his fellows is to damn the administration, complain about red tape, and suggest that the president ought to be fired. Snide jokes about the top-echelon administrators are passed along with vicious delight, while, in any given confrontation between administrators and professors, the members of the faculty almost invariably will assume the administration is wrong and the faculty is right.

College administrations vary tremendously in their approach to the question of democracy-versus-despotism. Some universities go on an orgy of democracy, allowing the professors to vote on almost everything. The result is, as I stated earlier, a cancerous growth of mediocrity. There are other universities wherein despotism has become tyranny, where every decision is referred upward for final resolution. It has been my observation that when a presidential despot retires, his replacement, the next president, generally will last only a year or two as the professors exercise their anarchical bent, once released from despotism. The second man to follow the tyrant generally has an easier time, for after a year or two of anarchy most professors sober sufficiently to want leadership. Extreme anarchy and extreme despotism, thus, are equally disastrous to the academic community. The best of all administrations, I have found, is the benevolent despotism. An administration genuinely concerned about the welfare of both professors and students, and with the power necessary to implement its decisions, can accomplish far more than any other form of rule.

THE PROFESSOR AND HIS ADMINISTRATION

Considering that most college presidents, vice presidents, and deans come from the ranks of college professors, the academic world has better administrators than could be expected. This, of course, is a generality, for there is an occasional poor president. But by and large I have found them to be a well-qualified group. Perhaps this is one area where the touted "Peter Principle" works in reverse. Men of ability rise above their level of incompetence; that is to say, they move upward from being professors to a level that challenges their abilities.

Few college professors and even fewer members of the public at large realize the clear line of authority in institutions of high learning. In public institutions, the state legislature charters the university and stipulates that all authority is vested in a board of regents. The regents, appointed by the governor and confirmed by the state senate, represent the public interest and are the sole body capable of making binding decisions for the university. They can delegate responsibility but they cannot abdicate it. And just as they can delegate authority, they also can revoke it. Most professors tend to think that once they get the authority to do something that power never can be taken from them. But all power rests with the board of regents.

84

Most members of boards of regents tend to come from among businessmen, professional men, and wealthy farmers. These are men of affairs who must be about their business; they cannot make every individual decision. Thus they hire a president and delegate most of the responsibility and authority to him. He makes decisions, but all of them are subject to board approval —or rejection. Any president whose decisions begin to be reversed by his board had better start looking for another position. He can do his work only so long as he has the confidence of his board.

In turn, the president must delegate authority, for his duties and responsibilities are too numerous for him to do everything personally. To help him, he generally has at least two vice presidents, one for academic affairs and one for financial affairs; one looks after the degree offerings of the university and the other handles the money. In addition, at a large institution there may be other vice presidents—perhaps one for student affairs, one for extension work, and even one for public relations (although the latter will generally have a fancy title that conceals the fact that he is a PR man). All these individuals serve at the pleasure of the president; they have no job tenure and can be removed at will. Thus they are under the direct control of the president, who himself can be fired at will by his regents. All these assistants relieve the president of the tedium of day-to-day work, allowing him time to do essentially a public relations job himself. The president represents the university to the public, makes endless speeches trying to explain his institution to the public, goes before the legislature to try to get more money, travels widely about his state, and, in general, promotes the university in every way possible.

Each of the major assistants to the president has his own crop of assistants. For example, the vice president for financial affairs had a comptroller, a purchasing agent, a bursar, and numerous other functionaries beneath him; while the vice president for academic affairs has a dean to administer each individual school. It is very easy to judge the quality of a school's administration by looking at these second-echelon officials. A first-rate president will hire first-rate underlings, while a second-rate administrator will hire third-rate men to work for him. A good man is not afraid of the comparison, while a poor one wants no competition.

Finally, the dean has department heads to control the individual disciplines in his school. The department head is the first member of the chain to have any tenure, for he usually retains his academic rank. He is listed as "Professor and Head"; thus he can be fired as department head, but not dismissed from the faculty. This then is the chain of command in the academic world: faculty member to department head to dean to vice president to president to board of regents.

And the typical faculty member tends to fear and envy everyone in the chain. He wants to be an administrator because he believes himself capable of exercising power. Salary is not as important to the typical academician as is status and the exercise of power; as one of the characters in "The Matchmaker" points out, "The difference between a little money and a lot of money is not very great." Getting a fifty-dollar-a-month raise is not nearly so important as a fancy title and a little money. Yet while the typical professor wants power and is envious of those exercising it, he also is extremely scared of anyone in power at any level in the chain—and more fearful the higher up the chain he goes.

For example, a friend of my graduate school days and now

president of a middle-sized university recently told me of one of his best faculty members who on entering the president's office became virtually speechless. He simply was unable to talk with any coherence in the president's office. It is not the president himself who frightens the man, but the office. I have seen this first-hand, merely as a department head. One of my best friends told me, shortly after I became department head, that he did not like to come into my new office to drink coffee; as he explained it, "I don't know why, but when I come in this office I feel like I did when I was a boy and my father called me in for doing something wrong."

Yet administrators are surprisingly human. Recently I visited the friend of my graduate school days who now is a university president. As he showed me his spacious office, I was curious to find if he had changed from the easy-going fellow I had known years before. "Don't you ever feel like a fraud sitting there?" I asked, pointing at his big swivel chair.

"Of course," he replied. "Anyone who takes a seat such as that is going to feel that way unless he is completely power mad. Sometimes I begin to think someone is going to stick his head in the door and yell, 'I caught you! Get out of here!' "

This same friend also explained how, as president, he is isolated and made to feel alone. At university social functions no one wants to sit with the president for fear others will think he is playing up to the boss. Even trying to eat lunch in the Student Union is a lonely exercise. And should someone sit down beside him, he generally is seeking favor or playing up to the boss!

The normal chain of progression up the administrative ladder is from professor to department head. Most department heads I know complain that theirs is a thankless task and that they want to be relieved of the onerous responsibility. The truth is that most of them would fight almost to the death to retain the power and prestige of the office; after all, if they find the duties too heavy, they can always resign as department head and return to being only a professor. In truth, most department heads aspire to become a dean—just as most deans want to be a vice president, and most vice presidents are looking around for a vacant presidency.

Yes, most professors fear and envy college administrators. Simultaneously they are afraid the administrator will find out about professorial incompetency and they envy the administrator's power. Most people in positions of power in colleges and universities know of the incompetence of their staffs; however, they have no one with whom to replace them but instructors fresh out of graduate school or else professors teaching at another institution—and equally incompetent or even more so. If there is real frustration loose in the land, the prime example is the college administrator, usually a good man trying to do a good job, but working with lazy students and incompetent professors—all the while trying to make legislators believe the institution is filled with excellent teachers and questing students.

ELITISM

It will come as no surpise to anyone who has listened to a commencement speech in the last ten years to know that a spirit of elitism has been fostered among students—and deliberately—by politicians. "You are the best-educated, smartest, healthiest generation in history," they say. Not so well known is the fact that many professors pander this same line to their classes. They do this through the same approach that politicians use: telling the students how smart, how well educated they are. And they do it by indirection. They have promoted the concept that "learning can be fun." Learning can be interesting; it can be rewarding; and it can be exciting. But it is not fun. It is work. Preaching the doctrine that learning *can* be fun soon leads to the student attitude that learning *should* be fun, implying that society has an obligation to make life a barrel of laughs. The result is an antiwork attitude which already is far too prevalent in America.

The words of politician and professor combine to reinforce the usual late-teenage ignorance; students of this age already assert their self-superiority. In short, too many professors pander to their audience and help the student to believe what his feelings of inadequacy have led him to assert: that he is smart and educated, that youth equates with eternal wisdom, that age equates with obstinacy and wrongness, and that the past has no lessons for the present. In this respect, I am reminded of Ambrose Bierce's definition, in *The Devil's Dictionary*, of a bigot: "One who is obstinately and zealously attached to an opinion that you do not entertain." Or of his definition of a bore: "A person who talks when you wish him to listen." The young wish to talk but do not wish to listen. They bore me.

This attitude of elitism on the part of students is dangerous, for it quickly breeds a belief in their nonresponsibility. They feel no obligation to family or society or country; in their quest for identity they place self above all those things that history has taught to be important. They feel themselves above everything. Thus they believe they are justified in using violence to enforce pacifism; they can shout down speakers with viewpoints in opposition to their own; they can throw beer bottles and trash out car windows while preaching against pollution (few communities have as much litter as those towns almost exclusively dependent on college students as a source of income). In short, their attitude of elitism leads them to believe they know better what is best for the country than do older or less educated yokels, and they intend to give it to the country whether it wants their solutions or not.

The truth is not nearly so flattering to these elitists, this best-educated, smartest, healthiest generation in history; the truth is far different from the fancy rhetoric of commencement speakers and classroom instructors. The young (that is, the eighteen-to-twenty-five-year-olds) constitute only some twenty percent of the population, but they are responsible for more than a third of all traffic fatalities. They commit almost half the crimes in America, and they use more than eighty percent of all illicit drugs. Thus while they shout the question, "What have you done to America?" to their elders, the same question might be asked of them with more telling effect.

Moreover, I would seriously question that this is the smartest generation ever. They may have more facts at their disposal and, thanks to television (given them by their elders), a broader range of visual information. Yet today's children have the same body chemistry with which to contend—the emotional instability that simultaneously clouds thinking and causes pimples. Their thought processes are no better than those of their parents, just as their level of intelligence is approximately the same. And, as do youth in all ages and cultures, they tend to see all issues in terms of absolutes, of blacks and whites with no shades or hues of gray; there are only good guys and bad, heroes and villains, in their conception of the universe. For example, the people of my generation when young cheered at the movies when the cavalry arrived to rout the Indians; today the young cheer the Indians and boo the soldiers. Both generations are equally guilty, it would seem, of thinking in terms of absolutes.

And today's generation is just as guilty of thinking emotionally rather than rationally. Just the other day, a student in one of my present classes was saying that the "establishment" made it impossible now for anyone to get rich. His solution was to redistribute the wealth; apparently he felt that if everyone did not have the opportunity to be rich, then all should be equally poor. When I informed him of studies showing there have been more self-made millionaires since World War II than in all the previous years of American history, he reacted first with disbelief and then with indignation. In short, he wanted to believe that the establishment was preventing his getting rich, not that his own shortcomings were holding him back.

Finally, today's young are guilty of something that the over-thirties were not. This is the age of the ugly! Ugly clothes. Ugly hair. Ugly manners. Ugly art. Ugly music. What a far cry from the elegant Viennese waltzes, the string quartets, the elaborate costumes of a century ago—or even the music, art, and clothes of two decades past. Today's generation showers its coins on musicians without training or talent—and the resulting noise is called genius. Tiny Tim is the epitome, the superstar, of the now children. And their highest praise is reserved for the "put on," the fraud, the fake.

The thoughts of youth may be long, long thoughts, as the poet told us, but all too often they also are full of inconsistencies, ignorance, and downright stupidity. The trouble with the young is not that youth is wasted on them, but rather that they rarely gain wisdom until it is too late for them: they have joined the ranks of the elders. Actually Robert Browning was closer to some eternal truth when he wrote, "Grow old along with me!/

The best is yet to be,/The last of life, for which the first was made. . . ." Youth was made to serve age, not be its master.

And all the beards and the long hair and the absurd clothes that some college professors grow and wear in imitation of their students only show that these men have yet to learn several hard facts. First, that everyone will age no matter how hard he fights the process; second, that age is superior in so many respects that the intelligent man prefers it; and, third, that the ridiculous philosophy that they stylishly pretend to believe is as bankrupt now as when it was originated—which certainly is not by the present generation.

Too often, however, the ranks of college professors are filled with former students whose antiwork attitude and whose beliefs of elitism precluded their ever doing something productive. So they stayed in graduate school to become professors. Now their beards and shaggy locks are but an advertisement of their ignorance; their ludicrous clothes but an indication of their unfitness to profess to the young.

POMPOSITY

Academicians tend to be a pompous lot—for exactly the wrong reasons. Let me explain. The more a person learns in any area of specialization or discipline, the more he becomes aware of what he does not know. Or to put this another way, it is easiest to write or speak strongly when doing so from a position of ignorance. The more you learn about any subject, the more you realize how complicated the subject is and thus become aware of how much you do not know. Professors, inasmuch as they study in great depth—all the way to their Ph.D. degrees —thus "sense" their vast ignorance. I use quotation marks around "sense" because this awareness of ignorance generally is at the subconscious level. Few of us are sufficiently strong to admit our ignorance to ourselves, let alone to our students. Thus when a student asks a question in class, he is a threat to the professor, for thereby the professor may have his ignorance exposed to public view.

The reaction of academicians to questioning, to what they realize intuitively is a threat, is varied. One of the standard answers is to refer to the issue as "too complicated to be reduced to ready explanation." The professor who uses this method simultaneously closes discussion while massaging his own ego; the inference is that the student cannot understand and that the professor does. Another method, and one frequently employed in the classroom, is to treat the student who asks questions with ridicule and/or sarcasm. "Don't you know that?" sneers the professor, implying that the questioner is a stupid jerk and that the professor is knowing and intelligent. When the professor's reply to a question is, "Everyone knows that," what he really is saying is, "I can answer this one." A final method is one entrusted to me when I was a graduate assistant. "When a student asks a question you can't answer," I was told, "simply announce you are glad the question was asked inasmuch as you intend to put that on your next test. The students then will find the answer in a hurry."

The vast majority of professors with whom I have talked do not realize why they react with pomposity or sarcasm or other defense mechanisms to the questions they are asked. Especially is this true of young professors, who tend to grade the hardest, give the most difficult tests, and react the strongest to questions; this is because they have not yet learned to live comfortably with their ignorance and because their egos demand that they appear omnipotent.

Yet it is not just the young professors who are guilty of this malady. Far from being aware of their ignorance, even within their own fields of specialty, most academicians go in exactly the opposite direction. They feel and believe and think they know the answers to everything in their own fields and virtually everything in all other fields. Thus they are a frustrated lot. They have ready solutions to all mankind's ills. Just ask them how to solve a problem of great complexity, and they can give immediate answers. Their frustration stems from the fact that they have the answers *but not the power* to implement them. This is why so many professors are involved in politics today; they realize that only through political power can they implement their solutions.

This explains why liberal academicians so loved John F. Kennedy. It was indeed to them an "Age of Camelot." At his inauguration Kennedy gave voice to the aspirations of these liberal academicians by calling for a "New Frontier" for the American people, and by having Robert Frost there to read a poem. Moreover, the new president did things with "style"— his rhetoric was flawless. He told his listeners that day not to ask what their country could do for them, but rather to ask what they could do for their country. To many Ivy League professors the answer to the question was obvious: go to Washington and enact their "solutions" into law; they knew what was best for the country and they intended to give it to the people whether the people wanted it or not. Thus a horde of "academic jackals" moved toward the nation's capital. Yet the Kennedy years, for all the charisma he exhibited and the professors he employed, were extraordinarily barren of real result. He promised much,

94

but delivered little. He had promised a raise in the standard of living, improved education, free medical care for the aged, higher social security payments, and improved civil rights for minority groups. Yet in his administration the only major piece of legislation was creation of the Peace Corps. His real political victory was a rules change in the House of Representatives that the liberal professors did not recognize as a victory, rather as a bit of mere dabbling in the dirt of politics.

Then came the assassin's bullet in Dallas, and Lyndon Baines Johnson became president. In November 1964, Johnson and his "Great Society" were returned to office—and the voters reaped the "reward." The drawling Texan promised to eliminate poverty; Congress responded by voting the Appalachian program. Next came the Elementary and Secondary School Education Act, giving aid to school districts, even to parochial schools. In July 1965 came Medicare, an adjunct to social security to pay the medical costs of the aged. And Congress, at Johnson's request, established a Department of Housing and Urban Development, with cabinet rank, to oversee the growing crisis in the cities.

Much to Johnson's surprise—and chagrin—these measures did not endear him to the liberals. The academic jackals who had come to Washington with Kennedy gradually left the capital to denounce Johnson. When he secured passage of the exact programs they had initiated and pushed—and these proved unworkable—they castigated Johnson, not their own failures—and then proposed even more unworkable schemes calling for the expenditure of yet more tens of billions of dollars. Any hesitancy on the president's part in espousing new Utopian schemes they interpreted as oppressive authority. Johnson had given them the fruits of their academic liberalism, but without the attendant cant of liberalism and without a Boston accent—and they turned on him viciously. Johnson spoke with the accent of the common man, which made him unacceptable to Brahman academicians.

The great irony of Lyndon Johnson was that he cultivated these liberal scholars and sought their benediction. He even hired more Ivy League graduates to work in the government than any previous president in American history. Yet the more he did, the greater the denunciation, bitterness, and invective —for the academic jackals considered the source more important than the achievements. The handiest club the liberals had was Vietnam, and they used this to destroy the man who had given them exactly what they had advocated.

And when these academic liberal professors forced Johnson out, which they did by calling out their storm troopers, the students, the result was the election of a moderate Republican. Thus the academicians were more frustrated than ever. They briefly had tasted power—and they liked it. Yet they could not sully themselves by engaging personally in politics and gaining the power they so loved. The result of all this has been a suicidal death wish within the Democratic Party, where the professors have had the most influence, a determination to rule or ruin—*all the result of professorial pomposity.*

FADS

Professors love to stress the individuality and the uniqueness of their occupation and their life-style. As a senior member of the tribe informed me in the early days of my career, "Academe is the last frontier of individualism. When you close the door to your classroom, you are entirely on your own. When you go to the library, no one tells you what to research. And when you sit down at your typewriter, the machine has nothing to say except what you tell it to." Perhaps, but it has been my observation that professors are given to fads in equal measure with other mortals, possibly even more so.

There are very few of them who teach with any uniqueness. I remember an explanation of the way physical education teachers perform their jobs in the public schools: open the doors of their offices, throw out a ball to the students, and tell them to play a game. The same is true of lecturing. In any given discipline there is a certain style of teaching. In my own discipline of history, the usual method is the lecture. In mathematics it is to demonstrate a new concept by working a few problems on the blackboard and then assigning problems. Rare indeed is the innovative teacher—or even the one who can really fill students with enthusiasm. Think about your own high school and college career, and if you can remember more than five dynamic instructors in the entire lot you are very fortunate.

Nor is there much innovation in researching and writing—if the professor is doing any. The odds are that he is not. Even among those who do "push back the frontiers of knowledge," there is a tendency to slavish imitation. Let's face it; there have been only a handful of books in the last half-century in any given discipline that have been of tremendous importance. Let the nation become excited about any given subject, however, and a host of scholars rush into print with ponderous tomes about that particular subject. For example, there has been a strong upsurge of interest recently in Indians and black Americans; sociologists, anthropologists, historians, the literary crowd, those in the fine arts, even the psychologists, have kept lumberjacks working overtime to cut down the trees needed to make paper for their effusions.

Naturally there is a reverse snobbery at work here also. At one convention, a historian informed me haughtily that, having authored a small work on the first Negro officer in the United States Army, some ten years previously, he had been working in black history "before it became fashionable."

Yes, professors are slaves to fads. Take the area of clothes— to say nothing of hair—for example. Not so many years ago the uniform for any professor with pretensions was the tweed suit (with curved-stem pipe attachment). And if the tweed jacket had leather patches on the elbows, then he had real status. For as brief a time as the fad itself, I saw Nehru jackets, followed by turtleneck sweaters. Now it is bell-bottom double-knit slacks of a color that only a few years ago would have denoted homosexuality, shirts of a pattern to embarrass any self-respecting Hawaiian, jackets of such nondescript appearance as to have come from the local Salvation Army store, and ties that narrow or widen at the whims of fashion dictators. All, naturally, with briefcase (preferably an attache case) attachment.

The current fad of concern for the environment has led to bicycle-riding by professors on a wide scale. Of course, there always were a few oddballs who rode them earlier, pretending to do so for reasons of reverse snobbery but really because of poverty, but now it is quite fashionable to ride the two-wheelers. Look on any college or university campus and you will find bicycle racks in sufficient numbers to rival a middle-class elementary school.

Possibly the most pervasive fad today, an indispensible necessity for the would-be intellectual, is sneering at television. "I never watch anything," you are assured at every cocktail party, office gathering, or coffee session. A question or two will elicit a stated exception, however; "Well, I do look at educational television occasionally," you will be told. At a recent small party attended by several members of my department, along with their wives, the sad state of television was the topic of conversation, and naturally both husbands and wives loudly declaimed that they never watched. I mentioned that I had enjoyed a recent special, whereupon several exclaimed they had seen it; this led to a further admission by most that they did watch specials. And when sports were mentioned, most of the husbands admitted to catching an occasional football or baseball game. Then one wife, without thinking, mentioned that she was intrigued with a character in a certain soap opera, whereupon the other wives wholeheartedly began discussing the rest of the characters. It occurred to me that for people who "never watch television," they knew one hell of a lot about the subject.

Finally I note the "My-country-may-it-always-be-wrong" syndrome so stylish among college professors. There has been some comment on this subject among the syndicated newspaper columnists in connection with the liberal-intellectual crowd of the Eastern Seaboard area, the crowd with which so many college professors identify in knee-jerk fashion. Rarely has history been so misused in our country as it is today. Distortions are deliberately made in order to make every event in our past seem to imply viciousness, greed, cupidity, stupidity, and culpability. A good example is the Mexican War; when in 1961 then-Attorney General Robert F. Kennedy referred to that war as one of the most disgraceful episodes in the American past, few historians bothered to correct him—and he was totally wrong. The textbooks of American history foisted on unsuspecting and gullible students at the public school and college level likewise refer to the Mexican War as something for which we should be ashamed. Yet more than eighty-five percent of the books written about that war do not make this charge, and recent scholarship has demonstrated conclusively that the blame lay more with Mexican politicians than with American greed.

Other examples could easily be cited to show the same thing. Perhaps this is because textbooks have historically been written principally by New England Ivy Leaguers whose Puritan backgrounds make them wish to confess their sins. *Mea culpa. Mea culpa. Mea culpa.*

Another possible explanation of this guilt complex is that it is popular with students. A debunking approach to teaching is almost a guarantee of student approval. The young feel that they knew more than their teachers in high school, and any professor who tells them that what they previously learned is wrong will rise in their estimation, for this is what their misguided minds have been telling them all along. In history, for example, a sure route to large enrollments is to dwell on the faults of the Founding Fathers; show that George Washington, Thomas Jefferson, and Ben Franklin had clay feet clear up to their waists, and the students will applaud. Yet people need heroes—it is part of the human constitution to be so—and the young, with the traditional heroes debunked, place posters of Ché Guevara and Chairman Mao (along with Howdy Doody and Humphrey Bogart) on their room walls. The professors thus are encouraging the dream fantasies of callow and naive and antisocial youngsters who feel that somehow, through some mystical process, the "bottom rail ought to be placed on top."

Yes, professors in the name of individuality and academic freedom are slaves to fads. Young instructors must build library shelves in their homes out of bricks and 2 x 12s to hold the books, few of which they have read and even fewer of which they understand. As they progress through the academic hierarchy, they must preach antimaterialism while grasping after higher and yet higher salaries. They must rail at seniority until they get enough of it to become the Establishment themselves. And when finally they get to the top, they suddenly discover that the system they have preached against and thereby weakened was pretty good; then they begin to talk about the "good old days."

FEELINGS OF SUPERIORITY AND INFERIORITY

As a professional group, college instructors probably have more feelings of inadequacy and inferiority than any similar group—which naturally they hide behind a mask of superiority. I recently saw this demonstrated at a national convention of members of my particular discipline, history, but the same scene probably has been played at conventions in every other discipline. At this convention, I overheard two individuals talking at a cocktail party, and from the talk I immediately deduced that they had attended the same graduate school simultaneously. "Where are you located now?" one asked the other. "I'm at Swarthmore," replied the second, his voice dripping pride because he was at a name Eastern school. "But," he continued, "it's not very good. The students are terrible." Here he was indicating that he obviously deserved better than his present location. He concluded by asking, "And where are you now?" The first man shuffled his feet in embarrassment. "Oh, I'm at Such-and-Such State University," he confessed at last, adding quickly, "It's just Backwater, U.S.A." The snide reference to the institution paying his salary was more than merely biting the hand feeding him; what the second gentleman also was saying was that he was better than his present situation indicated.

There are endless variations to this scene of inferiority hidden behind a mask of superiority. One obvious example is at the small obscure school where someone with good qualifications takes employment, only to be asked by several people, "What are you doing here?" The implication is that anyone with good qualifications would never take a job at such an institution; thus the person asking such a question is actually admitting his own feelings of inadequacy.

And there definitely is a pecking order of prestige among institutions of higher learning. Generally the order would go upward like this: the junior college is at the bottom of the list; next comes the small private school; slightly higher in prestige is the small state college, generally a converted teacher-training institution whose name has been changed to "college" or even "university"; above this level is the large private institution, generally one with a well-known football team; and near the top is the second-largest state institution; at the top of the heap within each state is the state university (*i.e.*, the University of Texas, the University of Arizona, the University of Wisconsin). The more prestigious schools are immediately recognizable by the company they keep in athletic conferences; the best ones are in the Big Ten, the Big Eight, the Southeastern Conference, the Western Athletic Conference, the Pacific Conference, and so forth. These schools historically have been the ones granting the Ph.D. degrees of the teachers at the lesser institutions. Thus a handy yardstick for measuring the prestige of a given institution is the athletic conference within which it plays and the number of departments on the campus offering the Ph.D.

Yet the professors at these schools likewise are unhappy.

102

There always is the Ivy League. There, ironically, football has been deemphasized—for the wrong reasons (reverse snobbery), but deemphasized nonetheless. Because these schools are the oldest, and therefore better known, most Southern and Midwestern professors aspire to reach the Ivy League. Only to learn that the professors in Ivy League schools are unhappy and want to move to the top institution in California (the University of California at Berkeley), where salaries are higher. But members of the faculty at the University of California at Berkeley likewise are unhappy; most of them want to be in the Ivy League!

In summation, then, we find that all professors are unhappy at their present institutions, claiming to deserve something better and feeling that another university has more prestige. Yet when you follow the trail of prestige, you find it goes in a circle!

Another form of proclaiming self-superiority (and thereby masking feelings of inferiority) is for the professor to decry the level (or lack) of culture in the geographical region around his present institution. "What clods these Texans are," proclaims an Ivy League graduate who was unable to find employment in New England. I have heard the same complaint about Oklahoma, Arizona, California, Maine, the Dakotas, the Pacific Northwest, and the South. Again what the professor really is trying to say is that he feels superior to the region, that he deserves employment in some more refined spot. Most people who make such comments actually are above their level of competency in being employed at all; they should bespeak gratitude to the region instead of complaining. Such comments always make me want to ask, "And if you are so good, why don't you move to some place more compatible?" Naturally such questions cannot be asked—they make too many enemies.

Today there is little feeling of superiority to be gained from academic rank alone. College teachers are assigned a rank that supposedly reflects their training, seniority, pay, and status; this moves upward from Instructor to Assistant Professor to Associate Professor to Professor. Instructors normally do not possess the highest degree (the Ph.D.), but above this level the rankings are more of seniority than quality; anyone teaching about five years as an assistant professor will be promoted to associate, and associates in grade for about five years will be promoted to full professor whether or not they work or publish. Even in pay I can detect little difference in the salaries of twenty-year veterans who have researched, published, and given good lectures as compared to the salaries of twenty-year veterans whose only accomplishment was to keep breathing. Thus rank has little real meaning—except that the lowliest assistant professor and the most senile senior member of the department all feel smugly superior to the dean, the vice president, and the president of the university. What I mean is that all faculty members claim superiority over administrators—while simultaneously seeking desperately to become one.

There are a few small benefits to being a full professor as opposed to an assistant or associate: more choice as to teaching hours, more pay, sometimes a smaller work load, better office furnishings. Just enough difference to make the Young Turks hate the Old Guard. Or as one old-timer commented to me, "I always hated the seniority system—until I got some of it."

Finally, within any given discipline there is a pecking order of prestige associated with various subdisciplines. The theoretical mathematician considers himself superior to the applied mathematician, just as the nuclear physicist believes his field carries more prestige than any other aspect of physics. Generally prestige is associated with the ability of the particular specialty to attract money. That area receiving the most grant money is the most prestigious.

But there are other aspects to this matter of prestige within the several areas of a discipline. For example, in my own discipline regional history has the least prestige because it is closest to home, while African history and Asian history are glamorous at the moment. The regional historian is made to feel himself the low man on the historical totem pole. Those specialists who deal in such intellectual subjects as New England village life or the revolutionary activities of some particular French commune in Paris in 1870 are known to refer to the study of the American West as "cow-chip history." Yet the human condition knows no regional or racial limits; a biography of one old rancher can speak to every man, everywhere, or it can be mere pages of provincialism sprinkled with ethnic coloration—just as can any biography. To try to establish some sort of pecking order based on area of specialty is ludicrous—and unscholarly. But it is a standard part of the scholarly world, one proclaiming feelings of inferiority.

Most professors have strong feelings of inferiority to begin with, stemming from their origins. Most of them are lower-middle class to begin with. Through hard work and by a close imitation of good manners, they gradually pull themselves sufficiently far up the ladder of success to overcome their hard beginnings. Yet instead of realizing that they are partaking of the Great American Dream, that theirs is indeed a success story in the Horatio Alger tradition, they still vaguely feel that someone will discover their lowly beginnings, and thus they go to great lengths to deny their own roots. In one department of history in which I served, we had a young chap join our staff in the field of Intellectual History. He came to us with excellent

105

credentials, a fine graduate school record, and high recommendations. When he arrived, however, we could hardly understand him, for his British accent was so thick as almost to be Cockney. We had on our staff that year a visiting professor, one so filled with years and honors that he did not feel constrained to observe the usual niceties. One day this senior professor stopped the young intellectual and told him, "Drop that damned Limey accent. You're nothing but another damned Redneck probably from upstate Mississippi." Later we learned that our senior professor's haphazard guess was correct; the young man *was* from upstate Mississippi.

Too many young professors try to hide their fears of inadequacy and inferiority behind one or another type of smoke screen. I recall speaking at a state convention in Texas, a meeting of the state historical society, whereat I saw at close range several young graduate students from the best-known university in the state. They looked like something a punch press had stamped out on an assembly line: each had on a smart, junior-executive-type suit, each carried an attache case, and none spoke with a trace of a Texas accent. Yet all were country boys from the Lone Star State, much as they might wish to hide their origins.

In this regard, professors are very similar to their undergraduate students. A British observer once noted that America is a land of rich students and poor parents. How many times I have seen students dressed in the height of fashion and driving the newest, most expensive sport cars, yet ashamed to invite their friends to their homes for fear their parents will prove an embarrassment. The family "mansion" described in dormitory bull sessions will prove to be only a three-bedroom, two-bath, brick home or even a small frame farmhouse. How many times have I seen students noted for their wardrobes and their fancy automobiles be greeted at commencement by parents driving a '55 Chevy pickup. Even more ridiculous is the student ashamed of parents who do not speak correct English or who do not dress "properly" or whose hands show evidence of hard work.

Such pretensions by students and professors about their origins mean that they are rootless. By definition a person who denies his roots is rootless. And rootless people, beyond being objects of scorn and pity, are dangerous. I have found, over the years, that a person who is ashamed of his origins is one who will be the first to knife you in the back, who holds few things sacred, who will try to climb to the top over dead bodies. Give me an educated Redneck every time in preference to the phony trying to sound like he just returned from Oxford. Or, as a friend recently wrote me, to describe the Urban Historian his department had just hired, "If only the library he unpacked had been any indication of his intelligence."

THE EDUCATIONISTS

An expression often quoted to ridicule professors is, "Those who can, do; those who can't, teach." There is a third phrase to add to this cliche that sometimes is quoted among academicians: "Those who can't teach, teach teachers." I realize that the professors of this discipline prefer to be called "educators," but in reality they are "educationists." And they are the laughingstocks of the academic world—which perhaps is like saying that they are held in contempt by the contemptible.

Professors of education hold their positions thanks to a monopoly they gained early through smart lobbying. In an earlier period of American history, when education was yet held in extremely high esteem, the educationists began lobbying to license teachers. This they achieved by saying that only by requiring teachers to have certain training could quality be assured in the public schools. Legislators in every state agreed with this thought and established standards for teacher certification that included certain courses in "Education." This, in effect, gave the educationists in colleges and universities the right to say who could and who could not teach, for by flunking students they could block them from employment. Thanks to this monopoly, every college has its Department of Education and every university its School of Education.

The tendency in departments and schools of education is to flunk very very few students, a trait that attracts the poorest-quality people into the profession. Those students who fail engineering and science and other difficult disciplines can always go over to the Department of Education and get a degree. And in the past a degree in education has been a guarantee of employment—not good employment, because salaries were terrible, but employment nonetheless. This is lamentable, for already the educationists were attracting only the poorest-quality students; the pay of teachers was so wretched that only the weakest students started with an education major. To retain these students who for one reason or another enroll for the education courses, the educationists traditionally have set the lowest possible standards and require the least amount of hard work to graduate: no foreign language, little science and math, and minimal coursework in the social and behavioral sciences.

In fact, the professors of education have even tried to make a virtue of their low failure rate by exclaiming with horror about the high failure rate in other disciplines. One educationist once

108

complained to me how terrible it was that forty percent of the students in freshman chemistry failed. I asked him what he thought would be a fair rate of failure, to which he replied "about ten percent." When I inquired if he would want someone of that arbitrarily passed thirty percent to be his pharmacist, he said I was being ridiculous and stalked away.

Evidence gathered by a national educationist organization has indicated that despite all the "methods of teaching" courses students take in college, more than eighty percent of them tend later to teach like some teacher they admired. Thus by their own evidence the educationists are accomplishing very little with four out of every five of their pupils. Perhaps this explains why their courses are so dull; they realize the futility of putting out any effort. Education courses tend to have little content, rather endless repetition of the same material no matter what the course title, and apathetic students filled with contempt for the professors.

Just how ridiculous education professors get was driven home to me once when one of them told me he conducted his classes by means of the "Democratic Lecture." Now those two terms are contradictory, for a lecture is by definition an autocratic thing. Yet he failed to see this point when I made it. By the way, this same professor also told me that in his first class after receiving his doctorate of education, he had a group of little-old-lady teachers in a summer course. He said he had them place their chairs in a circle for his democratic lecture, seated himself, leaned back, and began by saying, "Let's get to know each other better"—only to look down and see his fly open. (I have discovered that this is a secret fear of most professors—the open fly before a class. I have known professors who so fear it that they

109

make a habit of checking their flies just before going into every class.)

And, so reason professors of education, if a bachelor's degree in their specialty makes a good teacher, a master's degree makes an even better one. Thus they have lobbied into law in every state laws to force teachers back into school to take yet more of their meaningless courses. Every three or four years a teacher must return to take a couple of courses—unless he completes a master's degree. This master's degree almost invariably will be in education, for again it is easy and painless to secure: there is no language requirement, nor is there a thesis to be written—just take courses in education. I have heard people in small towns across America, in talking about some teacher, comment, "He (she) is very smart. He has a master's degree." Upon inquiry I find it is a degree in education—and thus only a guarantee of having warmed a chair three or four summers at some school, not of any intelligence.

The educationists have been able to get most of their theories put into practice in the public schools by their lobbying. Progressive education has become the battle cry that has seen every student being passed along—to the point where a high school diploma is worthless; it and fifteen cents will get the graduate a cup of coffee. It certainly is no guarantee that the holder is able to read and write, to do simple sums in arithmetic, or even to make change. Now the educationists would have us do the same in college. "Failure is bad for a student's personal development," they tell us; I wonder if lack of failure, no matter what the student's ability, is any better for personal development. The end result of this push to lower standards in colleges and universities has been and will be to place more stress on

110

acquiring graduate degrees before companies want to hire the student.

In this regard—the lowering of requirements—the educationists are in the vanguard of the academic world. Their undergraduate work certainly is the least-failed. And this has carried forward into their graduate schools. There also very few fail. And teachers who return to get a master's degree in Education then are encouraged, either by a desire to better their status in the public schools or to get an administrator's job or even to become college professors themselves, to go on to the doctorate of education (Ed.D.). Thereby mediocrity perpetuates mediocrity.

LADY PROFESSORS

The ranks of college teachers, unlike those of the public schools, have been almost totally male in the past. Probably this is because girls do not make good graduate students; the stress in graduate school is on individuality and is very competitive, whereas femininity in America has stressed noncompetitiveness and lockstep behavior. Moreover, the woman who pressed through to the Ph.D. found herself with a very limited supply of potential husbands, often unable to secure a job within the best schools, and regarded with suspicion by the public (the "why aren't you home having babies?" syndrome).

The type of young lady, in the past, who aspired to a professorial position generally was the sort who would insist on retaining her maiden name as a middle name if she married, even the type who would give her maiden name as a first name to one of her children. Few of them married, however, for they had grown hard and competitive in graduate school, and few men's egos can stand such competition. Government statistics bear out my opinion on this score: one-third of the young ladies who have received master's degrees in the past, and were unmarried at the time, never marry, while two-thirds of the unmarried women receiving a Ph.D. never marry. And those who do marry have an exceedingly high divorce rate if they are successful professionally, for they do not have time for home and family. The few happily married feminine professors I have known have been those with husbands who had abdicated from life; who, as one I knew put it, had become philosophers. Or as another I knew styled himself, "just a househusband."

Once the young lady does get her Ph.D., she finds herself discriminated against in hiring except in certain disciplines. For example, the ratio of women is quite high in music, home economics, and women's physical education. In all other departments she will have to work twice as hard to win promotion and pay raises from her fellow (male) professors. Moreover, the students do not like feminine professors as well as they do men. Boys hate to be bossed by women, while the coeds resent them because they cannot use sex as a weapon on them (well, maybe there's an exception with some of the physical education instructors). Yet in the in-fighting of office politics, I have seen several feminine professors who used neither intuition nor logic to gain more favorable teaching hours or better courses; they simply used sex as a weapon with the department head. A few honeyed words, an eyelash batted a few times, a couple of "Oh, you big handsome man" and the department head is eating out of her hand.

Lady professors do tend to become defensive, and with good reason. Last to be promoted, the lowest paid and teaching the least desirable courses, they have reason to complain. All except the home economics teachers. Almost without exception, these should be fired outright: male and female. (The males because most of them in home economics are frustrated females who need time to rethink their roles in life.) The home economics professors do more damage to marriages in the United States than almost any other breed. They train the coeds to cook on all the very latest equipment, which is donated by the manufacturers in the hope that the young graduate will fill her home with their appliances. They teach the coeds in interior decoration to expect very expensive furniture and very fancy homes. When these young ladies get married, however, it generally is to young men just starting out in life, men without the funds to purchase microwave ovens and fancy expensive appliances. They cannot afford designer furniture and original oil paintings to hang on the walls. Thus the coed who undergoes training in home economics, unless she is one of the rare ones who marries a wealthy husband, is going to nag her husband because she feels cheated. The result is an unhappy marriage. Home economics professors should train their students to cook on old stoves, serve appetizing meals from inexpensive cuts of meat, and make a small apartment an attractive place to live.

For these reasons I discourage most young ladies who talk to me about doing graduate work toward the Ph.D. They will find it frustrating in even more areas of their living than will the men. I am no male-chauvinist pig—I enjoy having a good-looking colleague. Rather, the reason I discourage women from entering the profession is because they will be unhappy and frustrated and with good cause. Only when females have complete equality in all segments of American life can they enter the profession and exclaim with the rest of us, "This beats working for a living."

And federal governmental regulations are doing everything possible to encourage this new day. Every year on college campuses, administrators have to send to Washington reams of reports stating the percentage of its professional staff that is female, as well as the percentage that is black, red, or yellow. Moreover, when a new employee is hired, the department head has to certify that he made an honest search for a qualified member of some minority group and did not discriminate on the basis of race or sex. This actually has made women Ph.D.'s in great demand, just as it has blacks, Chicanos, Indians, and Orientals. A professor at Columbia University recently summed this up for me; we were discussing the hiring practices everywhere this year, and he stated, "Everyone is looking for a black woman named Rodriguez!"

IV

PERPETUATING THE BREED

RECRUITING GRADUATE STUDENTS

Every university with which I am familiar is playing the numbers game. By this I mean they are madly seeking the most possible bodies. More students mean more prestige, just as they also bring in more money through tuition and state supplements. Thus, despite claims about standards of entrance, I rarely have known any student to be turned away from registering provided he was breathing and he had money in his hot little fist. Particularly is this true of graduate students. Universities are in a hard pinch owing to the creation of so many junior colleges; these can educate the freshman and sophomore at a fraction of the cost that universities can, and they are usually closer to the student's home. And the small state and private colleges are competing for the upper classmen—juniors and seniors—leaving the major universities only one real area without competition: graduate school.

And in graduate schools there are ever-growing enrollments.

An increasing number of applicants are indicating their willingness to study to become professors. Some do this because they think the academic life offers an opportunity for service; among today's idealistic types, this motive is strong. Somewhere during the years between twenty-two and about thirty, however, they tend to forget their idealism and become just as lazy as the rest of the professors. Others come knocking on the door of the profession believing they have superior ability to offer; they also fit right in, for egomania is rampant among academicians. Finally there are some who are attracted to the occupation because they are lazy. I know such was my case. I first decided to go to college and get a teaching certificate, work in the public schools, and lay around in the summer drinking beer and watching everyone else hurry to work. One week in the public schools convinced me I wanted out. So I worked on my master's degree with the intention of finding employment in a junior college where I could drink beer in the summer and watch everyone else hurrying to work. Just as I was completing my master's, however, I was offered a graduate fellowship to work on the Ph.D. I took this, thinking I then could get on at a college or university and lay around in the summer drinking beer and watching everyone else hurry to work. No one ever informed me that I would have to work all summer, every summer, in order to pay for the beer I drank, and I have had only two vacations in the last decade and a half.

The greatest source of supply for graduate schools is the university placement services—the agency at each university charged with finding jobs for its graduates. Those students who cannot get a job for whatever reason often decide to stay and work on master's degrees; thus industry's and government's rejectees fill the graduate colleges, along with those cowardly

116

souls who want to avoid the draft (at least this latter source has been large in the past few years of the war in Vietnam). Most of them are still unemployable or draftable when they complete the master's, so they stay to work on the doctorate—and end up by becoming professors. Thus society's rejects and cowards all too often become its teachers; the failures of life become the experts. They have no experience in politics or economics or even life itself, but they have become the instructors of the young in these subjects.

They stay in college to do graduate work because they are paid to do so. Few self-respecting students, however rich they may be personally, pay their own way through graduate college today. They expect—no, they insist—on receiving scholarships or loans, or assistantships or fellowships—or some combination thereof. Federal loan programs are available to the poor with a deferred payment schedule that waits for them to complete their work (and I read that a growing percentage of such loans are not being repaid). There also are myriad scholarships available to those who compiled good undergraduate records, while those who did poorly but cannot qualify for a loan can go to school under a federal program known as "work-study." Under this program they get about two dollars an hour for doing practically nothing, a boondoggle and swindle of huge proportions. And in the sciences, the professor who gets a grant to study the sex life of the Siberian tree toad has to hire a dozen research assistants (who do the work for him).

But by far the largest source of subsidy for graduate students is the assistantship. Here he is employed to teach even before he completes his work. In almost every department there is an introductory course with large enrollments; every major in that discipline has to begin there, while other students may have to

117

take it as part of their general-studies program. Such introductory courses carry very little prestige for the instructor (all professors want to teach only within their narrow specialties—meaning upper-division courses). Thus the graduate assistant or teaching fellow (the names are interchangeable) is assigned to teach one or more sections of these introductory courses at a salary ranging from $200 to $400 a month.

The public has contributed to making graduate assistants necessary. Immediately after World War II, there was a great hue and cry in the land to open the colleges and universities to everyone, to expand so that every American could have at least a bachelor's degree. The result was soaring enrollments, the erection of buildings (often hideously designed in WPA-Renaissance style), and the hiring of more and yet more professors. By about 1960, however, the spiraling costs of higher education forced colleges and universities to seek a cheaper means of instructing all those thirsting young minds. Thus administrators approved the employment of teaching assistants and teaching fellows, which pleased the professors who wanted to teach only specialized courses and to do their research.

Under the teaching-assistantship program, a regular faculty member lectures to the students one or two hours a week in the auditorium. Classes of 300, 400, and even more became common. Then the second and third day a week, the students meet in small groups—thirty to thirty-five—with the graduate assistant who is supposed to lead them in discussion (in the sciences, he meets them in the laboratory sessions). The regular faculty member never knows the students' names or even has to take the class attendance; a graduate student does that for him. And now the professor often is on video tape for his lecture and the students never even see him in person except as he walks across

118

campus to the student union for coffee; this is cheaper yet, for one professor's video tapes can be used to instruct a dozen auditorium sections of the same class.

The teaching fellow is more akin to a regularly employed professor in that he simply is assigned two sections of the introductory course and teaches them himself three days a week. He lectures them, he tests them, and he assigns the grades. Yet he is far cheaper than a regular professor in that two graduate fellows, teaching four courses between them and thus the equivalent of one full-time faculty member, make only $500 to $800; a full-time faculty member teaching the same load would have to be paid at least $1,000 a month.

There recently has been some public criticism of the employment of teaching assistants—complaints that these people do a poor job and that the typical freshman is cheated by never seeing a full professor. In the position I held until this year, I directed twenty-three of these teaching assistants and I can vouch for the fact that they do as good a job as regular professors. Perhaps even better, inasmuch as the typical graduate assistant is sufficiently scared actually to do some work. They tend to be more punctual, better prepared, and to hold classes for the full amount of time specified. And I believe that if the regular faculty here or on any campus was fired and the graduate assistants put into their slots, the student would not be able to tell an appreciable difference.

There are a few would-be professors who come to the campus where they think they might like to study to interview the instructors and to be interviewed themselves. When such a prospective graduate student shows up in my office, my standard question to him is, "What do you want in graduate school." When one says he wants "to drink from the font of wisdom, to learn everything," I try to discourage him from attending my classes. I had a student two years ago who, when I asked him this question, replied, "I want to get a Ph.D. so I can go to some small liberal arts college and be a resident intellectual." I did everything possible to run him off quickly. There is the occasional student who comes in and responds, "What do I want here? Why to get out as soon as possible." This is my kind of student. Him I understand, and him I can work with. I do not want to spend my time and energy with someone who wants to be an intellectual; he is likely to be in school here long after I am dead, for I know no way to train someone in being an intellectual. Just give me a student willing to work hard and who wants to get out and go to work for a living, and I will do my best to help him along. And if he is very smart, I will try not to hold him back too much.

Thus the graduate students arrive on campus every fall, dreams in their hearts and visions of Ph.D.'s dancing on their Christmas trees. They come for different reasons—too many of them for the wrong ones. They have myriad methods of financial support, but too many of them from the public trough in one way or another. Once enrolled and working as teaching assistants, they begin the process of transformation from student to professor, a process that is wondrous to behold.

THE TRAINING OF PROFESSORS

Entering graduate students often believe that intelligence is a requirement for doing satisfactory work. Rarely is this true! Genius and brilliance are more a handicap than anything else. Actually the *only* requirement for acquiring a doctorate is tenacity—the ability to hang on long enough to make the professors tired of you. (That and, I might add, a strong stomach for what one has to put up with.) Some of the dumbest people I have ever seen hold Ph.D.'s, people who could not find their own rear ends with a flashlight and a road map to guide them. Plodding, dogged tenacity will get a student across the stage at commencement far faster than brilliance, for dull and stupid professors always suspect intelligence. I heard two old professors once talking about this, and one of them said, "The most difficult thing in the world for a professor directing doctoral candidates to do is to stand aside and let a bright graduate student push through quickly. Once in a while I come across a student so intelligent that I simply try to stay out of his way and not slow him down too much, but, God, that's hard to do!" I can vouch for the fact that he was a rare individual; most professors cannot recognize brilliance, and when they do they hate it so much in someone else, especially a student, that they try to get rid of it instead of staying out of the way.

The theory of graduate school is that it teaches a student three things: (1) the facts, (2) how to find additional facts, and (3) how to communicate these facts. To accomplish the first objective, the student is required to take courses. The master's degree generally requires thirty semester hours beyond the bachelor's degree, and the doctorate an additional sixty semester hours beyond the master's. Inasmuch as thirty semester hours constitutes a typical year's work, the doctorate is the equivalent of three years' work beyond the bachelor's degree. This is not to say that the typical graduate student completes all this in just three years; quite the contrary. Most stretch the process out five, six, seven, and even more years. If he is employed as a graduate assistant, he must take a reduced load, just as other forms of employment slow him down. And even without the employment to slow him down, the typical graduate student takes about two years to do a master's and four to do the doctorate. Probably this is good, for it should give him additional maturity before he is turned loose on students full time; sadly it does not accomplish this always, for age is no criterion of maturity.

The student supposedly learns the facts that he needs to have at his fingertips in order to appear learned through coursework. He sits in narrow and specialized courses within his discipline until he begins to acquire these. However, he can never learn all the facts, even should he stay in graduate school for several dozen years, and thus point two is a necessity: how to find additional facts. This also is taught in courses, but of a highly specialized nature; generally these are called seminars. Here the student is told the methods of research, of footnoting, of compiling bibliographies, and of all the other gimmicks of scholarship. And in these seminars he has to write papers giving his findings; thus, in theory, teaching him how to communicate his facts. However, it is in the third purpose of graduate school that universities fail most often: communication. A few departments have courses on how to make a lecture and how to present one, but almost invariably taught by the poorest teacher in the department. And writing is a totally neglected phase of graduate school; few professors can write, hence few of them can teach the art; just as few of them really know how to teach and thus cannot impart any gems of wisdom on this score.

While the student is struggling through the coursework, he also is having to learn one or two foreign languages. The theory is that a reading knowledge of one or two foreign languages will better qualify him to do research. In truth, the language requirement is a farce inasmuch as very few students really learn to read or speak even one foreign language; about all this requirement accomplishes is to give employment to yet other graduate students in the department of foreign languages by swelling its enrollments.

Once the coursework and language requirements have been met, the doctoral student must pass a "qualifying" examination (at some schools, this test is known as the "comprehensives"). These are a major waste of time. Too many professors use the qualifying exam as a means of demonstrating their own wisdom rather than as a way to determine how much the student knows; this type of professor consults musty tomes within his field just before going to the examination and then asks very learned questions—to demonstrate his own wide knowledge rather than to ascertain what the student has learned. A professor once commented to me in candor, "Those exams are stupid. Anyone in the room could flunk everyone else there. Even the student, if allowed to ask the questions, could come up with questions the professors could not answer."

If the qualifying examinations are not for the purpose of judging the student, then what is their worth? They do allow the professors to massage their individual egos, and they indicate how the student will react under pressure. But the student has passed or failed long before he enters the room. By this I mean that in his relationships with each professor on his committee he has conveyed a message: "I work hard and I am interested in your specialty," or "I do not work hard and I am not interested in your specialty." If the professor believes the former, he asks questions that the student can answer; if the latter, he finds some obscurities designed to fail the student.

Overseeing the student during coursework, languages, and qualifying examinations is his director and his committee. Generally the director is the major professor in the field the student intends to take as his own major field. I have noticed over the years that students tend to be very much like their major professors in temperament, personality, and attitudes. I don't know if it is a matter of likes attracting or whether the student unconsciously imitates his major professor—probably a little of both. But students definitely do write like their major professors, even employ very similar teaching methods. Thus the professor supervising graduate students sees his own opinions reflected, thereby reinforcing his own belief in them. In fathering such intellectual children, the professor thus extends the scope of his influence—and contributes to perpetuating the dullness of the breed.

In accepting a graduate student, particularly at the doctoral level, the professor assumes an unspoken and unwritten obligation. It is his responsibility to find employment for his doctoral students, to help them move up the ladder of success, and even to aid them in publishing. And the student likewise assumes an obligation to his major professor: to speak well of him, to advance his name for office in learned associations, to fight the professor's enemies, and to laud the professor's friends. But as both professor and student are human, they both tend to forget their obligations very quickly.

Finally the student approaches his dissertation, again under the guidance and supervision of his director, aided by a committee (generally four more men) from the department. The dissertation, in theory, is a report on significant new research or else a report on a new approach to an old problem. In actuality it generally is an exercise in "transferring bones from one graveyard to another," as J. Frank Dobie once characterized it. By this he meant that the doctoral student hunted out obscure facts, wrote them into book form, and finally deposited them in the library where no one will ever read the end product. Granted, the good subjects have already been covered—a hundred years ago it was easy to find some major topic on which no one had ever written; still most dissertations are very poor. And yet the doctoral student almost invariably will send his work to publishers, hoping to see it printed into a best-seller. He works his way downward from New York houses to major university presses to local presses—and then buries it quietly. Several New York editors have told me that they do not read dissertations that arrive unsolicited inasmuch as ninety-nine percent of them are worthless. They merely are exercises in pedantry and obscurantism. Even when the topic is good, the writing generally is so poor as to preclude publication. I recently had a student do a biography of a major Midwestern figure, one known on the national stage, for his dissertation; the material was exciting and the possibilities excellent, but the student turned in a 500-page tome that put me to sleep in ten pages.

Once the dissertation is completed and accepted by the director and committee, the graduate student is given his doctorate—his license to go out and steal from the public trough. He now is a Ph.D., with all the pretensions, assumptions, and arrogance appertaining thereunto. I recall reading a story about a taxi driver passing by a university just as commencement was over. A student, diploma in hand, rushed out from between two parked cars, and the cabby almost hit him. "Watch out, you jerk," the taxi driver screamed out the window in anger. The student turned and waved his diploma, saying, "That's Dr. Jerk, if you please."

Dr. Jerk is a pretty good way of describing too many of these young new Ph.D.'s. I recall one newly hired professor who, at his first class meeting, was trying to put a map on the wall. To his dismay he discovered that he needed a screwdriver but did not have one. Finally he told his class that he would have to go to the departmental office to get one, whereupon a student came forward, took a dime out of his pocket, and used it to do the job. Later this professor was recounting the story to his colleagues, and as he finished he expressed total admiration for this example of what he termed "American ingenuity."

I am reminded here of the old story about the motorist who had a tire come off. Pulling to a halt at the side of the road, he noted that he was parked beside the state insane asylum. And as he began to inspect his tire, one of the inmates wandered over to the fence to watch. The motorist found that all the lug nuts had come off the tire. Turning to the inmate, he said, "Would you watch my car while I'm gone? I've got to go into town to buy some more lug nuts."

The inmate had a countersuggestion. "Why don't you just take one lug nut off each of the other three tires and use them on the one that fell off? That will get you to town where you can buy some, and you won't have to leave your car."

The motorist was astounded. "Hey," he exclaimed, "that's a terrific idea. I'll do it." He paused a moment to reflect, then asked, "But if you're smart enough to think of that, what are you doing in the insane asylum?"

The inmate had a ready explanation: "I'm in here for being crazy, not stupid."

Graduate school too often is just about the same; only too often we flunk out the original and creative thinker and reward the stupid with a certificate of his ability—the Ph.D.

UNDERSTANDING THE PROFESSION

Entering graduate students often are idealistic to the point of being blind to the faults of professing. They see the profession through the cliché of "rose-colored glasses." In fact, that is one of the things that attracts many young people to it today—the concept of service to humanity, uplifting the level of culture in America, and so forth. They tend to believe that professors live in ivory towers, that, isolated from the ordinary cares of ordinary people, they deal in "truth" and lead lives of great purity. What they fail to realize, in their youthful idealism, is that professors are human and thus subject to all the human frailties, vices, and faults.

And sitting in endless classes, both lecture and seminar, they still do not learn this fact. They see their professors as men of great intelligence and polish, men universally acclaimed for their wisdom. I still vividly recall the shock I received when I attended my first national convention and discovered that very few other professors had ever heard of the "great men" under whom I had studied.

In his informal discussions with his major adviser, the doctoral candidate should be made aware of the quarrels that go on among academicians and of the ins and outs of office politics. In short, his adviser should open his eyes to what the profession really is like. However, very few of them do—because very few of them understand the profession themselves. Many professors are too lazy to work at learning what the business really is about, while the others tend to play office politics at the intuitive rather than the rational level. Thus they are unable to explain the profession to their graduate students.

Graduate school, in theory, is a recruit-training depot for professors, but most professors fail in the role of drill instructor.

Therefore the typical young scholar has to learn his tactics on the field of battle. I would say that a major failure of graduate school is that it fails to teach the young scholar anything about human nature, which he likewise has failed to learn outside the portals of higher education.

In fact, graduate school often does exactly the opposite. I am thinking here of the final orals that the doctoral candidate has to undergo. This is after he has taken written examinations dealing with the subject matter in his major fields, and it is after he has completed his dissertation. The very last hurdle to be completed is known as the "final Oral Examination." This supposedly is where he defends the "thesis" of his dissertation. It is a holdover from medieval days when the potential young scholar was forced to sit publicly for a day at his university, and any passerby could ask questions that the candidate had to answer. Now the final oral examination usually is restricted to the members of his committee, and the subject matter almost totally is the dissertation itself. That is the theory. To me, however, it sometimes seems that the final oral examination today is used as a final screening device for would-be professors—that is, it is used to see if the candidate is smart enough to keep his mouth shut about this swindle called college teaching or else is dumb enough to believe the publicity about the nobility and hard work of the profession. Both these types of candidates— the very smart and the very dumb—pass. It is the ones in between who fail, those with enough intelligence to see through the garbage about college teaching but dumb enough to tell about it (and I suppose that pretty well tells you about the author of this book, doesn't it?).

Thus because the graduate student rarely learns the hard facts about the nature of the profession, he has to acquire this

128

knowledge in the course of his skirmishes once he is a professor himself. All too often he learns from his defeats. It is this failure of graduate school that makes me appreciate the few realists among my graduate students rather than the many idealists who wander in. Perhaps the reason I get so few realists is because these people have too much sense to become professors.

THE END PRODUCT

The shiny new Ph.D., fresh from graduate school, tends to be more similar to all others of his tribe than he would like to admit —no matter what institution he attended. Supposedly the graduates of the prestige universities are better trained, better qualified than their less fortunate brethren from the small institutions, but I have never been able to determine any major differences. All of them have the same attributes, which are:

1) *They are discipline oriented.* Their work has been so concentrated in one area of specialization that they tend to believe it the only field of study anyone with intelligence would enter. All "ologies" fall into two categories in their minds: "my field" and "the lesser disciplines." And because they see every problem in terms of their own particular specialty, they are unable to consider the difficulties of their administrators. They have no conception of the many and varied forces tugging at a university today (students, faculty, alumni, the legislature, the federal government, the public). And, simultaneously, they are unable to see the value of other disciplines, to learn from and to appreciate what the other disciplines might teach them about their own specialty.

2) *They have learned to hide their ignorance behind big words.* Going to college year after year does not make a man

any smarter, yet professors tend to forget that intelligence and education too often are entirely separate entities. Intelligence is something a man is born with or without, while education is merely something he acquires. "Educated fool" is an expression that well describes too many professors. They forget that language is a tool for communicating and that the bigger the words they use, the fewer people they can communicate with. Thus those four-dollar words of Greek and Latin extraction that they have so painfully memorized are more a hallmark of ignorance than of education when used on students or the public—or even on each other.

3) *They are intellectual cowards.* Every graduate student who would survive quickly learns never to go out on an intellectual limb. He should not be emphatic in his statements, oral or written, when he can equivocate. (Don't say "never"; say "rarely." Don't say "always" when you can say "usually.") Nor should he be specific when he can retreat into vagueness. Nor can he afford to be emphatic or specific in his friendships; if he makes an enemy of someone on the faculty, he might flunk.

4) *They are good at filling out forms.* The process of registering is an endless chore even for undergraduates. For the graduate student it is appalling.

5) *They are arrogant.* Every man needs some reason for feeling proud of himself in order to keep his self-respect. The new Ph.D. has a piece of paper, his diploma, which he thinks proves his superiority. I have heard academicians, about some nonprofessor who has dared write a book within their fields, say, "It's pretty good for someone without formal training"—implying that only those people, such as themselves, who have the Ph.D. are capable of thinking. This arrogance usually gives the young professor illusions of grandeur: today I'm at Podunk Uni-

versity; tomorrow I'll be at Harvard! Young arrogant professors tend soon enough to become cynical, disillusioned old professors.

6) *They are chronic complainers.* Endless griping is not confined to the academic world, but professors do tend to make a fine art of it. Any professor feels that as a practicing intellectual he is not sufficiently appreciated, that he is overworked and underpaid, that the country should turn to him for answers to all the national maladies. In short he expects his diploma to gain him respect, riches, and honor. When these are not automatically showered on him, he complains.

7) *They are dull.* How can they be otherwise when the academic world itself is so dreary. The men who trained them and the men whom they admire are dull. The lectures they have attended for the equivalent of seven years have been dull. The ideas they are repeating rarely come from within the academic community, but rather from people in science and industry, from government and the arts, or from the writings of antiquity.

In short, the graduate student who learns to be a narrow specialist, to bespeak big words, to fill out endless forms, and to be cowardly, arrogant, dull, and a complainer, is certified and sent forth into the world to be a professor.

131

V

INDIVIDUAL SURVIVAL

ACADEMIC QUARRELS

There really is very little excitement in the academic world. It is difficult for a professor with any experience to be stirred by the thought of giving another lecture, making up another test, grading his exams, serving on yet another committee. Granted, some professors appear to have been born sixty years old, while others already are dead but have yet to lie down; but even types such as these need something to stir their adrenalin occasionally, something to prove to themselves that they are still breathing.

The method chosen by far too many professors is to engage in petty and very personal quarrels. For example, I recall two distinguished, even nationally known, professors at a major Southwestern university who carried on a bitter feud for almost a score of years. At that institution each department had a chairman, but the full professors by vote made all major decisions. Once in that committee of full professors, the two scholars

I mentioned above got into an argument over a swivel chair costing $79. One jumped to his feet in anger, a man with more honors and renown than any fifty other professors ever attain, and shouted at the other, "B____, you're a goddammed pissant," and stomped from the room. All over a $79 chair that neither man really wanted.

These petty academic quarrels take many forms. As I mention elsewhere, one method frequently employed is to cut down your enemies in book reviews. I recall reading one review, written for such motives, no doubt, wherein the reviewer summed up his findings by saying, "In short, this 'revised edition' is worthless. Everyone connected with the production of the present edition should re-examine his motives—and hang his head in shame."

A more subtle method of cutting an enemy is to arrange a session at some academic convention whereat he will be damaged. Let me explain. Many sessions at academic getherings are a package arrangement. You go to the program chairman and offer to arrange an entire session; he possibly will accept the offer inasmuch as it relieves him of work. You get your enemy to give one of the papers; he tends to accept because reading papers at conventions brings prestige generally—it is something all scholars are supposed to do. But you arrange it so that the discussant—the "authority" who, after the papers are read, then critiques them—is someone who holds opposite views to your enemy. Thus he is professionally demeaned in public. The invitation you extended him to speak, which appeared to be an olive branch, turns into a hickory stick with which he is beaten.

And, of course, you talk about your enemies in a vicious way. If he is on the same campus, you tell students in office conference that the man is suspect of unscholarliness, that he is a

133

wretched lecturer, that his standards are unreasonable, and even that his ancestry is cloudy. Then, when students stop signing up for his classes, you pass the word publicly that the man is a poor instructor—as evidenced by what you have engineered. If he is not on the same campus but is in the same field of study, you tell your classes that his publications are "popular" and thus unreliable; especially do you stress this to your graduate students, for then they can pass along the same word to their own classes later and thereby extend your effectiveness in cutting the enemy.

Another way of doing the same thing is to talk to everyone possible at conventions and say, in effect, the same thing. "Did you see the review of his book?" you ask, if he has received a cutting review, implying that the review was deserved. You never cut him directly; rather you damn him with faint praise: "Oh, he's a pretty good scholar, I guess, but his classes are not well attended and the reviews of his books are not very good." And your audience will tend to believe you all too often because it is only too human to accept the worst about other people. Scholars are not very scholarly, I have observed; they smack their lips and roll their eyes in pleasure at reading a bad review —and even at hearing of them—and will quote them to prove a book is bad. "Have you ever read the book?" I have asked scholars who are citing a review to prove some work poor. "No," they reply, "I haven't read it, but the reviews of it are bad." How can any reputable scholar dismiss a book as bad if he has not read it? I find that very unscholarly. I do not object to bad reviews at all; every man who reads is entitled to be his own critic—but scholars should not accept one critic's evaluation of a book as "evidence" of merit or demerit. Book reviews are written for myriad reasons, and many an excellent book has

134

been cut for very poor reasons. And I have noticed that scholars tend to believe one bad review and to cite it in preference to four or five good reviews of the same book!

It is a petty life that depends on quarrels over office chairs and passing bad gossip to generate excitement—but such is the world of the scholar. I have observed many professors who fill much of their lives with just this type of thing, however. And yet the measure of a man is the greatness of his enemies. One who chooses to fight only small enemies has no real fight at all and can gain no stature by winning. To hate properly takes a great amount of time and energy. If the scholar is going to find his excitement in such quarrels, he should pick enemies worth that time and energy. And most scholars are not worth it. Thus if we judge the level of a man's character by the enemies he has, then most scholars are very small and petty.

OFFICE POLITICS

Academic politics are vicious—just as vicious as if money and power were at stake. Possibly academic politics are even more vicious than office politics in the business community because there is no way to tally a professor's books at the end of the year and see a profit or loss as a result of the decisions he has made. Our decisions and our maneuverings do not involve the investment of millions of dollars, but rather involve pushing ourselves and our departments into a more favorable position. For example, we want our particular courses and our departmental courses placed on the list of courses that all students are required to take (this list of courses is generally called "General Studies" inasmuch as all students have to take them). If we can get our courses included as a requirement, then the department will have more students, more faculty members will have to be hired, and we gain more stature on the campus. If our individual courses are made an optional part of General Studies, then we can petition for additional courses to be added within our specialty, and we get to teach nothing but advanced courses, not the freshman survey courses of little prestige.

Most academicians, I have observed, play the game of academic politics intuitively. They do not plan specific moves, but rather rely on intuition to tell them what to do in any given situation. Only a few, possibly about ten percent, play the game logically—reading the character of opponents shrewdly and planning moves that will get the opposition exactly where they want them. The potentially disastrous results of playing office politics was driven home to me very forcefully a few years ago when I was serving on a General Studies Committee and the Speech Department people petitioned us to place the introductory course in speech on the list of required General Studies courses. I had then (and still) a rather low opinion of speech courses and reacted instinctively and passionately by denouncing the petition. I suggested that speech courses were worthless and should not be forced on all students—which was exactly the wrong thing to do. The other members of the committee reacted negatively to my denunciation, knowing (intuitively) that their own courses were equally suspect, and were about to approve the petition. At that moment one member of the committee who had been silent heretofore spoke—logically—and killed the petition: "If we put speech on the General Studies requirements, we are going to have to remove some course because the number of hours required of all students is too long now. What are we going to remove?" That ended all thought of getting speech on the list because every other member of the committee feared that his own discipline might suffer if something had to be deleted. Logic is superior to intuition in playing academic politics.

But academicians will continue, for the most part, to play the game intuitively. Like actors they are so filled with their own egos that they cannot assess others with any accuracy. Thus their moves are based on what they would do themselves in any given situation, not on what the other person is likely to do.

In my younger days I was appalled at academic politics, for I thought professors ought to be above such things. I was aware that business politics could be ruthless, but I naively believed that professors thirsted for truth, not for departmental expansion or any other material thing. Sadly I learned the truth. Then came an experience of aiding in the publication of a book for the bishop of the diocese in which I then resided. In talking with various priests, I began to hear stories about the in-fighting that had occurred when the previous bishop had died and a move was afoot to name the new one. I concluded that if God's representatives here on earth are not above knife-wielding office politics, then professors certainly cannot be immune.

Fortunately for the young professor, he generally is not called upon to play the game until he has been around long enough to learn some of the rules. However, on occasion he arrives in a department where everything is done by vote and a schism exists that forces him to make a decision. One young colleague told me of his experience in this vein. With his Ph.D. just in hand, he was hired to teach in a department in a California institution. Just after he had unpacked his books and papers at his office, he was called into a senior professor's presence and was told, "I have eight votes, and the department head has only six votes. If you don't vote with me, you'll never get tenure, a pay raise, or a promotion." The young professor then learned that the department head had the power to fire him at the end of the year—and had fired his predecessor for not voting with him. "What could I do?" this fellow asked me. I shrugged my shoulders. We both knew what he could do: immediately begin looking for another job. A few times around the academic bramble bush and every young professor gets scratched before learning the ropes.

DEFENSE MECHANISMS

One way to explain what graduate students undergo in order to become professors is to say that no doctoral candidate should be allowed to graduate until he has the lenses in his glasses changed to a stronger prescription at least three times, he grows a coffee-cup extension on one hand, and his other hand becomes a cigarette holder. There is some truth to this statement inasmuch as graduate school is hard on the eyes and the nerves. But in order for such changes to be good training for a professorship, the final part of the expression should be changed from cigarette to pipe. A pipe can be a professor's good friend, for it is one of the world's best defense mechanisms.

When a professor is asked a question that he cannot answer or one that requires him to take a stand, he needs time to think. A pipe provides this. You can always pause to light it, for a pipe is constantly going out. Or, if you need more time, you can pour out the dottle, reload it, and then light it. And in extreme cases, you can do all that and clean the pipe. Perhaps it is this quality of the pipe—its usefulness in gaining time to think—that causes so many professors to adopt them.

And professors frequently do need time to think. You have to be prepared at a moment's notice to hide your ignorance on any given subject, especially if it is in your own field. You have to be able to camouflage your political and religious views or to hide your stand on collegiate matters. With your colleagues you must be up to the task of disagreeing with the administration's statements, but not in such a way as to stick your own neck out. For example, a "friend" will come to you and say, "What do you think of the president's latest statement?" You pause and comment, "I find it interesting." There's a word, "interesting," that has saved many a professor's neck, for it can be interpreted to mean either agreement or disagreement. The professor who would survive and flourish rarely takes a definite stand.

In fact, it is dangerous for a professor even to agree with a negative stand. Let me explain. Someone out to get you comes around and says, "Don't you think the president's latest comment is idiotic?" Rather than disagree, you reply, "Yes." Then this enemy goes to everyone else and says, "He says the president's latest comment is idiotic." The next thing you know, you are on the carpet.

Yes, a professor must have many defense mechanisms, a set of mental armor ever ready to protect himself from the volleys fired by both friends and enemies. Perhaps the best of all is double talk. And those professors who advance by working the system rather than by working themselves become masters at the fine art of double talk. And when they really become proficient at the art, they are made administrators.

Academic double talk is really very similar to political double talk—the same thing that is called "bomfoggery" among politicians: a lot of fancy rhetoric that means exactly nothing. It is the ability to say a lot of words yet actually say nothing. Every graduate student learns this technique. In taking my doctoral orals, my final examination before being certified a Ph.D., I was advised by a knowing soul to answer in this way: on those questions that I could answer, talk endlessly and fill the time; on those questions that I could not answer, try very quietly to shift the answer onto a topic where I did know something ("Your question reminds me of a similar subject. . . .").

For years I, along with all professors, have cursed the ability of college administrators never to give a straight answer to any given question. Yet, just a few months ago, I was invited to a small university campus to interview for the position of academic vice president. I was given a tour of the campus and the usual sales pitch about how excellent the school was and what fine prospects it had. Then came the formal interview with the screening committee. After about an hour—about halfway through the interview—I suddenly was struck by an appalling revelation that very nearly caused me to burst into laughter. I found myself engaging in administrative double talk—and I had not yet been tendered the position. Whenever I was asked a question calling for a point-blank answer, I would begin with "On the one hand . . .," then halfway through shift to "On the other hand . . .," talk fifteen or twenty minutes, and conclude by having never taken a stand or said anything that committed me.

Yet another frequently employed device among academicians to evade taking a stand or committing themselves is the questionnaire and the survey. When administrators ask for a report on something or other, we can always fall back on the necessity of a questionnaire. Regular professors question their students, while administrators do the same thing with the faculty. Two points come to mind here: we do this because administrators have a mania for quantitative data, and second-echelon administrators justify their existence by making up endless questionnaires and surveys. Because of the introduction of the computer on all college campuses, administrators have become obsessed with percentiles and numbers; ideas are suspect because they cannot be quantified, and the same with opinions. Thus we sample our students, ourselves, the public, anybody, in search of something that can be punched into a computer, the data "massaged," and some figures spewed out. The amount of this type of work, the making and taking of questionnaires, that a professor has to undergo is staggering. Rare is the week that two or three of these things do not cross my desk.

When computers first were introduced widely on college campuses, the general excuse for the expenditure was that it would speed up and simplify everything. My experience has been that every time a computer has replaced a human (as, for example, at mailing out student grades at the end of a semester or in registering them at the start of a semester) it has slowed everything down and/or fouled it up.

Yet the mania will continue—and worsen—for it is a marvelous defense mechanism. Ask a professor or administrator a "hot" question and he can reply, "Our surveys show . . ." This, of course, evades direct and personal responsibility on his part. A bad decision can be blamed on that impersonal item, the survey. If you press him hard, he then will retreat into double talk. This is because professors, being human, have discovered that the person who sticks out his neck on any issue is subject to having it chopped off. Survival is the name of the game here as in business, politics, and other facets of national life.

THE ROUTE TO POWER

The members of few professions are so obsessed with power as are college instructors. Simultaneously, the members of few professions are so hesitant about admitting to aspirations to power. In fact, one of the quickest ways to become suspect in the academic community is to admit to such an aspiration; greatness must always be thrust on you, never sought out.

There are two routes to power in the academic community, one having to do with your own campus, and the other with your particular discipline. If you wish to gain power on your campus, you choose the administrative route. Inasmuch as this method does not require publication or teaching ability, it is the one chosen most often by members of the academic fraternity. Thus the young professor who cannot lecture and who is unwilling or unable to write tries to move up the administrative ladder, which begins at the department head level. Once he gains this position, he has the power to recommend pay raises and promotions, and thus can affect the lives and fortunes of every member of his individual department. Moreover, advancement to department head immediately frees him of the necessity of researching and writing, for he can claim to be "too busy with administrative detail" to do these; and a departmental headship generally reduces his teaching level to just three hours per week.

Once he has achieved the headship of a department, the young professor trying the administrative route next tries to become a dean. This gives him power over several departments (pay raises and promotions), and it frees him totally from teaching. Finally, after a few years in a deanship, he makes application to become the president of some institution—indirectly, of course, so that again greatness can be thrust on him. Here he has total authority, checked only by his board of regents (who generally leave everything to him). Naturally there is a pecking order of status attached to the size of the school he heads, so the ambitious young president who begins at a small institution will administer it for four or five years and then try to become chief administrative agent of a larger and more prestigious school.

The other route to academic power is through the individual discipline, and here power is more indirect. Inasmuch as you will have no say over pay raises and promotion, you have to achieve power through means that can affect these two items —chief among which is the power to get people published. If you can gain an editorial position, you have direct say over an outlet for the endless articles and books that professors produce —and that is raw, blunt, plain power. The most enviable position in this business is the executive editor of some academic journal; here you do not have to do the actual work (that is done by the managing editor), but you do make the decision as to what gets into print in that journal, just as you can direct certain books to specific reviewers and thus make them favorable or unfavorable at your personal whim. As executive editor you have the power without the dirty work. Still, the managing editor can make some of these decisions (those not made by the executive editor), so he likewise is courted by professors at conventions. I have seen hungry young academicians standing in line to get to talk to some editor not worth the time of day.

Another great source of power is the publications committee at your university (provided it has a press). Generally the editor of every university press has to have the approval of his publications committee before he undertakes to issue a new title. And on the publications committee, the member from the discipline in which the manuscript is written generally has life-and-death power to make the final decision. He has this because the other members of the committee want that same power over books within their disciplines, and thus they scratch each other's backs.

Another great source of power within a specific discipline is the ability to place people on programs at the academic conventions. If a professor can get on the program, generally his expenses to that convention will be paid by his home institution, and he gains status with his colleagues. So the position of program chairman for each convention becomes a power struggle as you try to get yourself or one of your friends named to fill it. In fact, you fight harder for this than you do to name the president and the other officers of the organization; those offices carry only honor, whereas that of program chairman carries power.

Another source of power, one at your home institution, is a seat on the speakers' committee. At every college and university a multiplicity of speakers are needed for banquet and luncheon addresses, for clubs and groups, and for what often is called the "Fine Arts Series." Being asked to speak at some distant institution makes a professor more appreciated at home, especially if his expenses of travel are paid and he receives some honorarium for speaking. And to be paid to speak is the height of professorial ambition. Thus if you can get on the speakers' committee, you can throw some honor and money to friends and potential friends, you gain influence within your discipline, and you incur the obligation of being asked elsewhere yourself.

Another route to power within your discipline, one that requires time and work, is to train large numbers of graduate students. If you graduate several dozen M.A.'s and Ph.D.'s, they in turn will extend your reputation and influence over the years. They will tell their thousands of students that your books are excellent; they get you on their campuses to speak, often for pay; they sometimes can get you on the program at conventions; and they advance your name for high and honorific office within the organizations of your discipline. There are several men I have known who have become president of the American Historical Association not because of publication or excellent teaching or any other major contribution to the discipline, but simply because they trained so many professors that their students were able to secure the office for them. I feel certain the same thing has happened in other disciplines.

Thus if you want power within the academic world, particularly in some specific discipline, the most certain way is to gain the authority to get people on programs and/or published. Perhaps this is why some professors push their home institutions to host an annual convention within their disciplines and then to publish the papers from those meetings. If you can reach a position where your decisions are so meaningful that program positions and/or publication results, you will be amazed at the number of friends you will have within your discipline.

TOWN AND GOWN

Faculty relations with people in the community wherein the college or university is located often are very strained, especially if the town is small. In large cities the professors gain a certain anonymity; their foibles and peculiarities can go unnoticed, so much of what I write in this section relates to faculty-townspeople relationships in smaller communities. In these, familiarity indeed breeds contempt. There the professor generally looks with disdain at the "provincial rednecks" in the area, while the townsmen call the professors "nothing but a bunch of damned communists" or "just plain fruitcakes." Thus "town and gown" are at loggerheads, their relations characterized by mutual misunderstanding and mistrust.

I should point out, in fairness to professors, that local merchants and businessmen contribute a great deal to this problem. I have heard these townspeople complain endlessly about professors having no town loyalty; they go to the nearest big city to buy their automobiles, furniture, appliances, and other items of major cost. They do this because they can save a considerable sum of money on such purchases; for example, a couple of years ago I bought a new car for $400 less in the city just fifty miles away than I could have purchased it locally. When I mentioned this to the local new car dealer, his response was, "Go buy it there if you can save so much." Too many of the merchants in these local college towns have enough business to make them about as much money as they feel they need; thus they do not hustle to make more money. And those professors who do buy locally only make the area businessmen feel superior: "That dumb professor paid too much," they say. "I sure stuck it to him." Thus the professor who buys locally gets laughed at, while the one who goes out of town is hated for his lack of civic pride.

Most university administrators are aware of this problem, as are some town leaders, and the two get together frequently to try to improve the relationship. Professors are encouraged to join local civic clubs—the Kiwanis, Rotary, Optimists, Lions— and the University will open its cultural events to local citizens. Dramas and musicals that come to the campus are promoted in town, and some of the recreational facilities on the campus are made available to townspeople. Sometimes this can cause a problem, however. For example, if the university has the only

146

swimming pool in town, it is pressured to make it available during the summer to everyone; then along comes some local entrepreneur who builds a public swimming pool at which he charges admission, and immediately he begins a campaign to close the university's pool to public use, saying that the university has no reason to compete with private enterprise. Local merchants also will pressure the university to keep prices in its student union as high as or higher than the prices of local restaurants and movie houses. These local citizens are all for use of public facilities until they see a way to make money off the students and faculty; they then become ardent capitalists.

In a wider sense, town and gown come into conflict on a statewide level, and there is a desire on the part of university and college leaders to promote a better understanding of the academic community. They do this, in part, because they want a healthy budget passed by each legislature—and thus to get pay raises for themselves and the faculty—and in part they do it to increase enrollments. In fact, much of what passes for public relations work at the university is a device for recruiting students. College officials hope that some of the Future Farmers of America and the Future Homemakers of America, who come to the campus to hold their annual meetings, will return in the fall as students. Even the Interscholastic League meetings are for the same function. These are held, so administrators will state publicly, for the purpose of "putting scholarship on a par with athletics." Thus, in the spring each year, they hold academic contests, each high school sending its best students to the campus to compete for individual and team points. Again the unstated hope is that these students will want to come to that particular college or university.

And there is the Alumni Association on each campus. Its

147

purpose, in theory, is to provide information to the old grads about their alma mater, to keep them abreast of developments and changes at the hallowed halls of ivy. In reality much of what the Alumni Association does is designed to get the ex-students to donate money to the school; these donated funds are prized by administrators because they are not budgeted line-item appropriations and thus can be used for many purposes—even for paying for trips to recruit athletes and for under-the-table subsidies to athletes. (Here I should add that much less of this goes on now than ten or twenty years ago because the various athletic conferences fight it so hard.)

Graduations are another time when administrators try to push public relations. Parents who come to the campus to see John or Mary graduate naturally are happy with a school that would award a degree to their dumb child, so they are in a generous mood. And the alumni are called to meet, with special preference being given to the older ones; they get their pictures taken individually with the president, not because administrators give deference to age but because it is hoped the old person will leave the university something in his will.

Graduations also are a time when honorary degrees can be conferred on millionaires—who hopefully will give a bundle to the school. This practice has been so widely misused that many state institutions by law cannot give an honorary degree; they get around the intent of the law by giving "distinguished service awards" and "distinguished alumni awards" to people whose merit is measured by their bank balances as much as anything. Private colleges and universities, who are not subject to a state prohibition on giving honorary doctorates, pass these out wholesale; in fact, many of them would go out of business if it were not for "selling" doctorates.

And finally there is athletics as a source of promoting the institution. One professor told me recently he could tell this was a school with high standards and much prestige when he took the job because we were members of a nationally recognized football conference. I am reminded here of Ambrose Bierce's definition, in *The Devil's Dictionary,* of two words placed side by side: "Academe . . . An ancient school where morality and philosophy were taught"; "Academy . . . A modern school where football is taught." Today any college or university is known by the athletic company it keeps; some very poor schools have strong reputations not because of their academic programs but because they have winning football teams. And a good season on the gridiron can have a direct, immediate, and telling effect on the next legislative appropriation. Thus many professors who sneer at athletics and carp that money is being poured into getting winning teams actually are receiving high salaries because of those same teams.

If there are conflicts between town and gown, the reason is not altogether one-sided; the townspeople do contribute to it by gouging professors through overcharging. But without doubt the major reasons for town and gown conflicts are to be blamed on the teachers at the institution: they feel superior, they sneer at uneducated or less educated people, they do not work hard for the tax money they are taking, they fail at public relations. In short, they are guilty of everything with which I charge them throughout the rest of this book. These relations can be improved only when faculty members learn that degrees do not equate with intelligence. As my father used to say, "An education does not make a man any smarter; it only enables him to hide his ignorance behind big words."

FACULTY WIVES

Show me a young lady capable of playing bridge for three straight hours while complaining all the while about the lack of intellectualism in her friends, and I can then show you a potentially fine faculty wife. A look at faculty marriages will prove the old adage that husbands and wives tend to become more and more alike over the years. Thus any woman with an accurate knowledge of the academic world would do well to spurn a proposal of marriage from a present or potential academician.

Most faculty wives come to that position from lower-middle-class origins. And most of them, just like their husbands, do not want to admit this. I recall twenty years ago, in the service, hearing a group of army noncommissioned officers' wives discussing the servant problem in Japan. They spoke of how difficult it was to recruit and retain trained servants with the assurance of people born to command lesser mortals—when, in truth, most of them were from cold-water walk-up flats in South Jersey and had never had servants before in their lives and never would again. Faculty wives tend to remember the old plantation manse if they are from the South, or the townhouse apartment and suburban estate if from a great city—after the rural ones have adjusted to plumbing and the city ones have learned that every apartment on earth does not have rats and roaches.

Most of these naive children approach the academic community scared stiff, fearful of some blunder of etiquette that will expose their humble origins. I have known one or two fortunate young women who actually rejected proposals from academicians because they so feared exposure of their origins by formidable old dames married to full professors. Those who do marry into the ranks are immediately invited to join a faculty wives' club (sometimes there is a newcomers' branch). In such clubs the young wives tend to cluster together for protection and warmth, while the older members likewise form their group. This is done under the pretense of separate interests—*i.e.*, the young ones want to talk about their babies while the older ones want to talk about gardening, a vacation somewhere exotic, or retirement in the sunshine. Actually the young huddle together out of fear of exposing their ignorance, and the old biddies are then left by themselves.

In the faculty wives' club the young ladies are introduced to "culture." (The speakers who make the ladies' club circuit must be among the world's most saccharin and cutesy, with not a drop of culture among them.) The newcomer learns to push cookies around a teacup saucer and even to drink tea, which generally she hates, but she eats and drinks and smiles. After ten or fifteen years of such tea-and-cookie affairs, when finally she gets comfortable in this routine, she continues to eat and drink and smile—and still hates it secretly. Fearful to be themselves, because this might "hurt my husband's chances for advancement," faculty wives tend to become carbon copies of one another and of their husbands while speaking of the individualism of the academic community. And in their anxiety to conform, they invariably overdress. At the start of the academic year, late in August or early in September, furs are often in evidence (rabbit or fox stoles).

And the young faculty wife learns to attend plays she does not understand, attend concerts she hates, even to go to poetry recitals. They become cultural maniacs in the hope of camouflaging their origins. As they get older and their children need them less, they organize bridge groups, golf foursomes, myriad hobby groups, and serve on endless committees. Every meeting

151

of the faculty wives' club demands a decorations committee, which naturally must come up with a "theme" for that meeting, a theme carried out in the centerpieces on the tables and the nametags given those in attendance. They attend the lunch with frozen smiles, drop names of the dean's wife or the president's wife, try to help their husbands, overdress, eat student union food (never known as excellent cuisine), listen to a cutesy speech, and go home to explain what a good time they have had.

In the words of the Roman poet, Decimus Junius Juvenalis, "They make of life an anxious joy. . . . All these condemned." Fortunately the younger breed is slightly different. Some of the modern types, liberated women, are rebeling to the extent of not joining such farces. Instead they gather at each other's homes for beer parties, barbecue in the back yard, and the usual cutting word games that women of all ages play. At least this is more honest than the gentle blood-letting of the faculty wives' club groups.

FACULTY ENTERTAINMENTS

Every fall at most colleges and universities there is a reception of the faculty by the president, who is joined (doubtless with little joy) by one or more members of the board of regents, his vice presidents, and assorted other flunkies. This can be a formidable experience to the young professor on his first job. I recall vividly the first of these affairs I attended, but not for the event itself. Rather I remember it because we, my wife and I, were taken to the affair by my department head and his wife; when Mrs. Department Head got out of the car, she changed from the comfortable shoes she had worn in the car to a pair of formal shoes—and proceeded through the reception line wearing her shoes on the wrong feet.

At these affairs today I see every level of dress. Young liberal militant professors express their disdain for the system by showing up in mod clothes better suited to a discotheque than to a faculty reception; they come with hair down to their shoulder blades, men and women, with beards instead of ties, and with sandals instead of shoes. I have even seen an occasional pair of blue jeans. At the other end of the political spectrum I have seen full professors show up at these semiformal events in tuxedos, their wives in evening gowns and furs (despite the fact that most of these events are held in September when the weather is hot); after all, most faculty members and their spouses get few opportunities to go formal, and they stretch a point wherever possible to pull these clothes out of mothballs. And there are the retired faculty members and their wives, dressed in items fashionable fifteen years ago, while the middle-aged professors and their wives come in their Sunday suits.

After passing through the reception line at these events, the professors and their wives get a cup of punch and some cookies —both of which are designed to help the sale of acid neutralizers. Invariably the punch is a bilious shade of green or a hue of dog-puke orange, while the cookies probably were made at the local cement factory. People do their duty with this stuff, however, getting it down, smiling all the while and trying to make conversation with the dean, the department head, and anyone else who may help get them a bigger salary or a promotion.

Then they are free to go to interest groups. Available are such hilarious diversities as dancing in the ballroom or bridge in the student cafeteria. Most go home, where they find better fun watching reruns on television.

153

Another form of masochistic punishment that passes for entertainment on campuses is the "fun" organized by the faculty club. The faculty club usually is an old-guard organization whose board of directors sponsor three or four dances a year—yet another chance for the wife to wear her high school formal; and they hold an athletic dinner at the start of the fall semester to allow us to meet the happy warriors who will represent us on the gridiron (always it is better to have this before the season than after, for the coach may not be around in the spring). Finally, the faculty club will sponsor a family picnic in the summer; at this they serve half-done barbecued chicken instead of overdone student union food. In fact, the summer picnic is the only one of these events not held in the student union; after all, the president wants all functions held in the student union to help pay for the building, and the students avoid "their" union as much as possible for their social events.

Then there are the functions slated by the several schools. The dean of each school feels compelled for some reason to inflict one of these social events on his faculty at least once a year.

These generally feature some atrocious singing by someone from the Music Department; the faculty of most music departments consists mainly of people who studied music endlessly but who did not have enough talent to make it professionally. They think they must inflict something "classical" on the audience to prove they have culture and talent. The result almost always is a selection rendered off-key to an audience that mostly does not know the difference—and definitely does not care. Both audience and musicians would be happier with selections from the Grand Ole Opry than from some classical composer whose work requires talent to render.

154

Following the music comes the after-dinner speech. The event is not "scholarly" unless everyone is put to sleep by someone addressing himself to a heavy topic. In fact, it was at a College of Arts and Sciences annual banquet that I first noted the ritualistic aspects of public speaking. This last spring I was at yet a different meeting, one on another campus in this state, at which the Music Department was to furnish the entertainment just after the meal. Two "girls" labored us for forty minutes, singing way up in the roofs of their mouths—off-key—in the name of entertainment. Then the invited speaker went for one hour and fifteen minutes on something about a bit of civil rights legislation in 1875. The chairs got awfully hard before that evening was over—and almost cured me of wanting culture.

Finally there are departmental functions. These are more intimate dinners, served naturally in the student union, featuring the usual inedible food and the terrible speaking that characterizes all faculty entertainments. And at these the politicking is even more intense, for it is here that most faculty members think they can help themselves—and their wives can see a one-to-one relationship between professor and department head.

My best advice to young scholars is to attend these functions only until you get tenure, and then avoid them like the plague. You will find the food better at home, the company more stimulating at a corner bar, and the intellectual fare more challenging on daytime TV soap operas.

CONCLUSION, EPILOGUE, AND AFTERWORD

The dean looked the faculty in the eye and commented, "Too many of you think education today ought to consist of a student sitting on one end of a log, and you sitting on a pillow on the other end of the log." Here he was rewriting Aristotle (or was it Plato?), who said that education ideally consisted of a student sitting on one end of a log and a professor sitting on the other. Because of the widespread abuses that have crept into the professorial system, more and more professors are going to start sitting on bark again, not on the feather pillow to which we have become accustomed and to which we feel entitled.

During the boom years of the mid- and late 1960s, we in the college teaching field came to believe that the good times were here permanently. Job offers abounded, each offering a higher salary than the previous one. Scholars moved here and there, living off the taxes of the land; we were in such short supply that it was a seller's market, and we could do what we pleased, teach poorly or not at all, rail at the establishment, all with impunity.

156

We laughed as college and university administrators coped—or tried to cope—with the problems besetting higher education: nonnegotiable demands from minority groups, the sexual revolution that demanded open-door dormitories with no hours set, drugs, homosexuality, student control of the board of regents, professorial control of the university, lawsuits by students over grades and degrees, faculty lawsuits over academic freedom to teach communism or socialism, and the overriding issue of granting tenure to one and all. Not only did faculty members laugh at administrators facing these problems, but many of the instructors did everything possible to intensify the confrontation with authority at all levels.

The bubble has burst at last. About 1970, the job market dried up, and with it student unrest began to simmer down. Legislatures began to take a hard look at what was being done on university campuses, and a new concept was born: holding professors accountable. Accountable for what they teach, how much they work, and how tax money is spent. Suddenly the long-haired fuchsia-shirted young Ph.D. found himself unable to get a job, any job, even one at a low-prestige junior college, unless he became concerned with his personal appearance (that is, he got a haircut and donned sensible clothing); he needed to concern himself with academic affairs rather than political causes (that is, do his job of teaching subject matter rather than political and social attitudes); and it helped if he was married and had children and if he indicated a willingness to join a service club and become active in civic activities.

Once these young men have cut their hair, laid aside their social causes, and begun teaching, they are finding that tenure is more and more difficult to acquire because of abuses of the privilege; that salary increases are not coming each year simply

157

because it is the anniversary of the last raise; and that some work is demanded of them, some accountability for the money they are receiving from the public trough. Even some of the older, more liberal professors are learning that the actions of the few are hurting all of us, that one riot at Berkeley or a spree at Columbia, when shown on national television, has an effect on the actions of the legislature in Nevada and Iowa. This discovery is making more conservative professors than all the logic in the world, for while the liberals are quite generous with other people's money, urging that it be passed out wholesale for any idiotic cause, they become very concerned when the money involved is their own. They will spend my money and your money, but they want theirs.

Accountability is not popular among the Young Turks, but it is accomplishing results. Yet what I have said earlier in this book is not suddenly a thing of the past. These abuses are very much with us yet, for most of it is ingrained and protected by tenure. And when the young professor is granted his job security in the name of academic freedom, too many of them promptly begin to abuse it; others, motivated by a martyr complex, keep grinding away at the establishment. And laziness among yet other professors will be with us always. I stand by my comments, assertions, and opinions despite the changes that have been wrought by the tough job market.

In making these assertions and comments, I have used the word "I" throughout this book. This is a most unscholarly pretension, but it is appropriate inasmuch as the book is highly personal. It is my view of the world of the academic. I admit to being guilty of many of the faults described to you, the reader, as I would never admit them to my colleagues. I also admit that age is catching up with me. I tend not to talk so forcefully in my

lectures, to moderate my pace, to reduce the amount of time I put into my duties. I find it hard to continue to believe that committees accomplish anything concrete, that training new professors will bring fresh breath into the profession, even that professional activities will be reflected in my paycheck. I guess I am saying that I have made the transition from Young Turk to Old Guard, and that I now am a member of the establishment, whatever the hell that is. I am a full professor with tenure and find my job secure.

Perhaps it is only that I am in the midst of middle-age restlessness that motivates my writing this book. And my advancing years were made known to me quite forcefully a few weeks ago when I was preparing to teletape a lecture in American history. I was searching for a song popular during the Mexican War era entitled "Green Grow the Lilacs." I was unable to secure a record containing this song in the university library or among my friends, so I decided to make the ultimate sacrifice and buy a copy. The only recording of the song with which I was familiar and which I thought might be readily available was a long-playing album of historic songs issued by *American Heritage,* the magazine of history. I went to the record store in our student union and asked the long-haired clerk, "Have you got the *American Heritage* album of songs about American history?"

"American Heritage . . . American Heritage," he mused. "Man, I don't believe I know that group."

This group called professors is a difficult one to know well enough to lump together. I admit that I have been guilty of a little overstatement in places, but that is a necessary part of satire. And I know that some professors who read this thing will disagree with my comments about the profession—which is fine so long as you bought the book and did not get it as a free review copy. Finally I admit that there are some very good professors, who are underpaid at any salary. Let's see, now, there's me and . . . You know, I think I will keep on professing. At least the level of competition is low, and it does beat working for a living.